Praise for the Poetry of Daniel Mark Epstein

On *No Vacancies in Hell* (1973)

"He creates a rhetoric combining the voices of character, of wonder-filled child poet, and of mature image maker. His people we recognize as the people of all our streets; these poems are local histories, specific in their detail, but are universally experienced."—*Bookman's Weekly*

"Like Ezra Pound in large swatches of *The Cantos,* Epstein jolts us into an awareness of histories we didn't know existed and which he finds important. . . . 'The Assassins' is so fine I hesitate to extract from it. . . . I enjoy his monologues for their triumphs and for the aesthetic problems they present."—Peter Klappert, *Parnassus: Poetry in Review*

"The smoothness and impelling momentum of a wide strong river with no choppy rapids or hysterical white water, remarkable balance, for the poetry is at once conservative and radical, old-fashioned and fresh. Dan Epstein is a roiling mass of contradictions who speaks calmly."—*Baltimore Sun*

On *The Follies* (1977)

"Here character sketches, several personal poems, and a beautifully executed 'Nocturne' are balanced by a twenty-eight-page four-part narrative ('Rodempkin') ironic in tone, elaborately patterned by long hanging lines, and (in spite of the ironies) essentially moral statements."—*Michigan Quarterly*

"Alternately sucking on the dry, dead bones of humor and spitting out natural street phrases, the author is a second-story poet with a deft ability to steal your attention."—*Library Journal*

On *Young Men's Gold* (1978)

"Epstein is basically a poet of love and celebration. His greatest strengths are wit and tenderness, a kind of energetic muscularity, and great technical skill."
—*Washington Post*

"One of the best books of poetry to appear during the seventies. . . . Quite possibly the best long poem since *Howl.*"—*Baltimore Sun*

"The first poem in *Young Men's Gold* is called 'In a Free Country.' An adaptation of the sonnet form, it is as good a love poem as has been written in this or any other century. . . . Each poem seems to be a new beginning, a sudden attack into new territory and new combination of words. They are like separate star-shells going off along some Western Front of the imagination."—*New Republic*

"*Young Men's Gold* seems to me as stirring and disturbing as almost any narrative poem to have appeared in this country since Jeffers and Frost passed on." —David Mason, *The Poetry of Life*

On *The Book of Fortune* (1982)

"Epstein's work is vivid, controlled, and wonderfully varied in approach." —*Publishers Weekly*

"There is hardly a word in his unrhymed and often unmetered poetry that isn't the most precise word he could have used. . . . Often his poems reflect practical concerns that have almost disappeared from poetry, such as tensions between the technological world and the natural world. This is the subject of a narrative poem cast as a letter from naturalist John Burroughs to Thomas Edison about their friend Henry Ford's obsession with things mechanical."—*United Press International*

"In the fine, contemporary writing that celebrates the natural world, nothing is more powerful than this."—Donald Hall, *National Review*

On *Spirits* (1987)

"In poem after poem of his fifth and newest collection of verse, Daniel Mark Epstein shows how miracles, surprises and perhaps even spiritual dimensions pervade things and people's lives. . . . Everything in the world of this poet reveals a cornucopia of hidden surprises, with spiraling processes embracing and infusing all."—*Chicago Tribune*

"By now Epstein has become one of our most assured craftsmen; poems in this book range in technique from prose-like syllabics to a new variant on the folk ballad in the third section of 'Raphael,' perhaps the most spectacular of a whole series of poems dealing with artists, poets, and dancers—though certainly the greatest tour-de-force of the set is his 'Homage to Mallarmé' in which three prose poems by Mallarmé are freely adapted into, respectively, five-line, nine-line, and four-line stanzas."—John Unterecker, *Michigan Quarterly*

On *The Boy in the Well* (1995)

"Some of the finest lyric and dramatic poems he has ever done. For its intellectual breadth and technical polish of its best poems, this collection merits high praise. Though I have not thought of Epstein as a lyric poet in the past, this new volume's final poem proves me wrong; fittingly, 'Helen' is a dramatic lyric, its humor both wry and knowing."—David Mason, *The Poetry of Life*

"Epstein is a truly outstanding poet. I admire the flexibility that can produce compelling short poems like 'At Poe's Grave' and 'Helen,' a fully justified sestina in 'The Inheritance,' and a fine story-poem in 'Solomon and the Four Winds.' I am grateful for his artful openness, his power to touch the heart."—Richard Wilbur

"For all his absolute clarity and purity of diction, Daniel Mark Epstein raises dark winds of the spirit and starts echoes from the past. The rocky deserts of biblical Israel and the meadows of Greece are both his native ground. Each poem is a masterfully wrought structure of fine phrasing, sharp imagery, and metrical liveliness."—Guy Davenport

On *The Traveler's Calendar* (2002)

"Biographies of Aimee Semple McPherson and Edna St. Vincent Millay have won Epstein greater renown, but his best writing is his mythically and historically haunted poetry. . . . Epstein's new work, while lovingly leavened with three sonnets celebrating his son, expresses the sorrows of the middle of life's journey with near-Dantesque poignancy."—*Booklist*

"Epstein's work has always been characterized by storytelling clarity and formal elegance, and driven by a restless curiosity about the ways in which people handle crisis. . . . *The Traveler's Calendar* is a strong, accomplished collection. Full of lived and contemplated life, it is both honest and abashed about our efforts to manage the brief time we have in this world."—Floyd Skloot, *Southern Review*

On *The Glass House* (2009)

"*The Glass House* . . . is, to my mind, the best of all his many published books of poetry. As usual there are many moments of poetic tour de force, with the flow always leading to an enlightening and often compelling outcome. Also, as usual, these poems must be read; not quickly scanned. The rewards for such attention are immediate and memorable."—Roxie Powell, author of *Kansas Collateral*

On *Dawn to Twilight: New and Selected Poems* (2015)

"The arrival of a volume of new and selected poems by an accomplished poet is a much-anticipated event, as was Daniel Mark Epstein's *Dawn to Twilight,* which rewards the reader from the early poems through the most recent, confirming that Epstein is a superb poet and translator. [This] selection of lyric poetry makes me want a second volume—this one with the translations and longer poems."—Miriam Kotzin, *Per Contra*

"Epstein's editorial decision invites us to reconsider the lyrical dimension of his work, that may have been overshadowed given the attention that the longer, narrative and dramatic poems received, particularly in the 1970s and 80s. . . . Recalling the extended metaphors of Frost's short lyrics . . . poems such as Epstein's 'The Secret' grow more complex the more we read them. These complex dynamics are extended in Epstein's magisterial new poems."—*Kenyon Review*

"At the heart of Daniel Mark Epstein's poetic project is a sense of time's dizzying velocity. Sometimes it's pictured as a conflagration. But despite the encroachments of time (conveyed with wit and pathos in newer poems such as 'The Cataract' and 'The Clockmaker'), we find throughout Epstein's work a steadying impulse to meditate, celebrate, sing."—Mary Jo Salter, author of *Nothing by Design*

"This extraordinarily lovely and moving book is a testament to the achievement of a major American poet."—Adam Kirsch, *Rocket and Lightship: Essays on Literature and Ideas*

constellations

Also by Daniel Mark Epstein

PROSE

Star of Wonder
Love's Compass
Sister Aimee
Nat King Cole
Edna St. Vincent Millay
Lincoln and Whitman
The Lincolns: Portrait of a Marriage
Lincoln's Men
The Ballad of Bob Dylan
The Loyal Son: The War in Ben Franklin's House

PLAYS

Jenny and the Phoenix
The Midnight Visitor
The Leading Lady
Jefferson and Poe
Somerset Tavern

TRANSLATION

The Trinummus of Plautus
The Bacchae of Euripides

constellations

the collected poems of

DANIEL MARK EPSTEIN

LOUISIANA STATE UNIVERSITY PRESS
BATON ROUGE

Published with the assistance of the Sea Cliff Fund

Published by Louisiana State University Press
lsupress.org

Manufactured in the United States of America
First printing

Designer: Barbara Neely Bourgoyne
Typeface: Adobe Text Pro
Printer and binder: Sheridan Books, Inc.

Jacket background image taken from *Atlas Céleste de Flamstéed* (1795), New York Public Library Digital Collections.

Library of Congress Cataloging-in-Publication Data

Names: Epstein, Daniel Mark, author.
Title: Constellations : the collected poems of Daniel Mark Epstein / Daniel Mark Epstein.
Description: Baton Rouge : Louisiana State University Press, 2025. | Includes index.
Identifiers: LCCN 2025018339 (print) | LCCN 2025018340 (ebook) | ISBN 978-0-8071-8477-6 (cloth) | ISBN 978-0-8071-8535-3 (epub) | ISBN 978-0-8071-8536-0 (pdf)
Subjects: LCGFT: Poetry
Classification: LCC PS3555.P65 2025 (print) | LCC PS3555.P65 (ebook)
LC record available at https://lccn.loc.gov/2025018339
LC ebook record available at https://lccn.loc.gov/2025018340

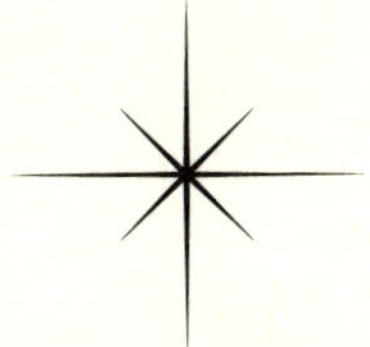

For Monsignor Joaquin Bazan

CONTENTS

New Poems

From *Dawn to Twilight* (2015)

From *The Glass House* (2006)

From *The Traveler's Calendar* (2002)

From *The Boy in the Well* (1995)

From *Spirits* (1987)

From *The Book of Fortune* (1982)

From *Young Men's Gold* (1978)

From *The Follies* (1977)

From *No Vacancies in Hell* (1973)

PREFACE

This collection is the work of more than half a century. It reminds me of a painter's layered impasto or a palimpsest (a parchment that has been erased and written over again), more orderly on the surface than in its older depths. So, I have chosen the modern convention to present the books in reverse chronological order, presenting the new poems first, then the more recent books, then the older books, back to 1973. As one turns the pages, the reader goes deeper into the past, discovering the foundations of the new poems in the old. Read the poems in any order; it is likely the newer poems will offer themselves more freely, making way for the earlier ones.

This book is mostly distinguished from my selected lyric poems, *Dawn to Twilight* (2015), in including narrative and dramatic poems, such as "The Assassins," "Letter Concerning the Yellow Fever," "The Testament of Isaac Lakedion," "Lafayette Square," and "Letter to Thomas Edison from John Burroughs" that are essential to the thematic structure of the eight individual volumes that I published before 2010.

The poems "Young Men's Gold" and "Rodempkin," long poems meant for stage presentation, are not included, nor are most of my translations.

New Poems

The Last Station

Like a traveler seated backward on a train
who sees almost nothing until it's passed him by,
he has missed his childhood and his children's.
His youth is a blur, and middle age an illusion.

And what looms large diminishes rapidly
to a vanishing point before he can name it:
a forest that never occurred as separate trees,
a woman waving goodbye at the last station.

Meadows and fields bloom and yield so quickly,
the seasons' colors run together. Even the mountains,
much greater than the land, bow
to lowly hills that fade away into the sky.

He nods to the snow that veils all such dimensions
so gently, and sleeps, a ghost adrift in drifting snow.

Vision in February

Under the vault of light blue
morning sky, on an ash-gray hill,
I saw the image of a horse,
gigantic, the sinewy neck and flank;
and all from mane to hoof clear-cut,
cast against the broad side of a barn.
This shape loomed before I saw the horse
standing below, golden—yet trivial.

Little was left of winter but bare bones.
I missed my parents, long dead,
and grieved for my distant children.
I saw the shadow of tree trunks and twigs
and crows, who look like shadows,
before I glimpsed the things that posed for them.
Such a brilliant morning in late winter
when I saw the stallion's lofty silhouette—

I felt like I might ride that shadow
into the real world beyond the hill
into fresh wind, midday and early spring
beyond this melting world into the next.
Who have I become that I can see
the shadow of the horse, the clouds, the tree,
man, woman, all things dear to me
before I see the living things themselves?

Who have I become now that the echo
of cries and laughter precedes the living voices?
What deep valley has created such a chamber?
Years have passed since I was on horseback.
Surely time has come for me to mount
again, and spur the horse to a full gallop,
clear that split-rail fence in the far field
and leaving this body, fade into the forest.

Silverfish

There's a hole in this page
the size of an eyelet
you poke in cardboard to let
the sun and moon slip through
so you can view the eclipse
without going blind.

I did not make it,
no, the little window
was the work of a silverfish.
But let's make the most of it
to see and be seen as if
this was our fondest wish.

Peering between the lines
now I see you
daydreaming as people do
when no one is watching.
It is a god's-eye view
from where I stand,

eternity on either hand
and your face before me
in a moment of candid beauty
like the cracked seed of creation
from which swirled
the unity and variety of the world.

The Watchmen

I think of you, Andromeda, and the shepherds
who lay on the hilltops, sleepless in love,
counting sheep and connecting the dots in heaven
as nature tempered the wind to the shorn lamb.

I think of you, blameless beauty, to blame only
because others bragged of your beauty:
your mother the queen, Cassiopeia, comparing
both of you to the ravishing Sea Nymphs;

and nothing would appease their jealousy
but the virgin herself, naked, chained to a stone
there to be eaten alive by the sea monster.
What happened then, the hero's flashing sword,

the girl's tears and shame, his famous words:
"There will be time enough for weeping,
but the time for risk and rescue is all too brief";
the serpent slain, his nostrils spouting water

and blood—an ancient poet tells it all—
and how the bride descended from the rock.
But none of this tale is written in the skies.
There is nothing but a scattering of lights

that if you are half asleep or full of longing,
might be taken for a naked woman:
here a gem for an ear, there one for a nipple,
a string of jewels for a leg and the great star

where thighs meet, Beta Andromedae.
I think of the genius of those guardians
who in their loneliness drew on the sky.
Few watchmen now have shepherds' crooks

and all the visible stars are accounted for.
    I think of the mortal patience
that made the constellations long ago
    and the immortal patience that made the stars.

Lost and Found

for Cindy Kallet

She sang with a voice for all seasons—
summer's ember, autumn's wind—
and fingers that danced on the strings

of a guitar that knew her mind,
for they had grown up together
and taught one another to play

sea songs and seabird's cries,
love longed for, lost and found.
Blessed with ears for such sound,

and a wise and supple contralto,
she sang and then took a bow;
she came and she went away.

And leaving, she left behind
more than an echo, a tone
that colors our whole house

from roof beams down to the ground;
and also, this glittering thing
I picked up in her wake,

long after the ship had sailed:
a reflection on the dark sea,
the slightest hoop of gold

slipped from the pierced ear
that hears what is hidden from us.
It gleams like the crescent moon

on a clear night in October.
Now who but a sorceress
would hang the moon in her ear?

Memorial Day, May 25, 2020

I never met Timothy Clover, and wondered for years
if I had made him up, if my memory had played a trick
on me, or if he had made himself up, like a Phoenix.

He published a poem in our high school literary magazine
when I was a sophomore, and then vanished without a trace
of his existence apart from the name. What's in a name?

In his case it seems like the perfect poet's name or the name
for the perfect poet, Timothy Clover, a fragrant pastoral image
like something out of Virgil, a tuneful shepherd or goatherd.

If poets are born and not made, this one, with such a name
was surely born to be a poet. And if the young man made it up
then he was born to make a poet of himself as most of us

struggle to do. Anyway, it was a very big high school
and I never met him or anybody who had. I just remember
the evergreen name above the title of a poem and a few lines:

"And when she asked me why I was always looking down
on these spring days when the sky is so clear and blue,
I explained to her that on such days the sky of May or June

looks the same from horizon to horizon as we walk under it
while the ground changes at least six times." Timothy Clover
wrote that and I remember it more than half a century later.

That makes it real poetry. Whether the youth himself was real
or not was a mystery. I imagined him, tall and blond and thin,
ethereal like Shelley, his head in the clouds and stars,

an ear cocked for the Muses who always called on him first;
feet that scarcely touched the earth as he strolled beneath
that perfect blue sky of a Maryland spring, an astral spirit.

But today is Memorial Day and we are sheltering in place.
Walking under the wide sky of May and looking down
upon the delicious changing earth beneath my feet,

I think of Timothy Clover. Real or made up? Fact or fiction?
With time on my hands, curiosity and a search engine,
I mean to find out. It takes all of five minutes online.

LIONEL TIMOTHY CLOVER: born January 10, 1947,
died May 22, 1968; Vietnam War Era Casualty: Hostile,
killed in action, "multiple fragmentation wounds, mixed

rocket and mortar fire, Tay Ninh Province." In other words,
the poet was blown to pieces. A few more clicks and then
I learn he was drafted, left behind a wife, and son,

one year of age. The day of his death was five days after
the Catonsville Nine, priests and poets, burned the draft files
with homemade napalm, the same spring Martin Luther King

was shot dead on his balcony, and race riots set our cities
on fire, and students closed Columbia and the Sorbonne.
On his tombstone in Fredericksburg, the inscription reads:

"LIONEL TIMOTHY CLOVER / Poet / Lived for Peace / Forced
Into War." So he did make it up, the name that is, by deleting
his first, "Lionel," (from the Latin), which means young lion.

Virginia Round-Leaf Birch

I think of Briar Rose in the castle tower
    seized by brambles as was promised
by the twelfth witch over the golden plate

denied to her jealous sister—who prophesied
    the girl would prick her finger on a spindle
and die. Instead, she slept a hundred years.

Despite the king's precaution, henchman's care,
    burning every spindle that could be found,
she wound her way up the spiral stairs

to a corner where a hooded woman bent
    treadling the last spinning wheel in the land;
picked up the tapered stick with its silver pin,

shed blood and fell into the arms of sleep.
    Sleep took the castle and everyone in it
while hedges of thorns and thickets wrapped around.

Many a prince risked life and limb, and lost,
    trusting the legend she was alive in there,
until the term was served, the spell was broken.

Behold the king and queen upon the throne,
    the cook asleep in the kitchen, flies on the wall,
and the lovely girl stretched out in the cold tower.

One kiss, and soon the kingdom was awake.
    An eon slips away. Our children's children
are grown and rule dominions of their own

with new histories and laws and fairytales.
    And I have seen bold wonders in my time,
from sea wave spindrift to spiral galaxy,

by sunlight and starlight fixed in turn
    on mountain peaks and prairies, lakes and bays,
halos, auroras, ice fields, and volcanoes,

chimeras real and chimerical in these woods.
    I have read in the gospel a strange tale
of Lazarus sleeping and Lazarus come from the dead,

and hear that somewhere in Virginia or Tennessee
    today there grows a curious tree
first seen and catalogued a century

ago, then lost to mortals, judged extinct:
    a birch with heart-shaped leaves
and black bark with the scent of wintergreen.

Dutch Comfort: Thoughts on a Figure of Speech

1

It's a comfort that things are no worse:
that the wind that blew out the lights
and toppled trees, knocked none down on your house;

that the storm came on a Sunday
when there was no work to be done;
a comfort that the cough is not a cold,

the cold not pneumonia, or if it is,
it is not the viral kind that kills
or if so, it is not you or your beloved

who dies but some stranger or enemy—
good riddance—or someone very old
whose life is a burden. And if death comes,

as it will even to you, it is a comfort
to think that death is easy, a destination
longed for, Heaven or a wayside inn

with fire on the hearth, the company
of old friends before bedtime, or at least
a dreamless and untroubled sleep.

2

My grandfather came from the Netherlands,
a cabin boy on an English rigged windjammer,
then a master mariner, and as good a man
as ever smoked a pipe or swam a mile
across the roiling flood of a tidal river;
honest as the day is long when days were long.
No prude or moralist or paragon, he
lived as well as he could, let others live
and knew to hang his head when he'd done wrong.

So I never understood such figures of speech
as "Dutch Courage," which comes only with gin,
or "Dutch Nightingales" for singing frogs,
or "Dutch Music" for any kind of racket
made by a drunken party where some are singing,
some shouting and fighting or pounding the table
with fists and mugs. How can it be
that the nation of Rembrandt and Anne Frank,
windmills, dikes and tulips, and my grandfather,
became synonymous with all that's false?
Some ancient war for mastery of the seas,
a feud over trade in pepper, wool, or lace
turned our English tongue against the Dutch.

My grandfather taught me how to sing and fish,
to play gin rummy, drink a glass of gin,
and drive his four-door Ford when I was ten.
A Dutchman head to heels in wooden shoes
he wore around the house and in the garden—
not the best, and not the worst of men.

The Gulf Stream

His broken mast, his hatch and rudder
are lost in the rampant sea. The black sailor
naked but for ragged pants, and a charm

of bone or moonshell dangling from his neck,
lies on the tilting deck of his wrecked sloop,
his noble head erect, in profile gazing

not at the pale-blue funnel of the twister
that seems to suck the sea into the sky;
he does not regard the faint schooner

hovering behind him on the white horizon,
the square-rigged masts, dim bowsprit,
a futile specter of salvation or deliverance

from one pitiless port in nature to another.
As sharks circle and nudge the listing wreck,
each one a study in cruel triangles—

the hunting mouth and dental fin, the scythe
of a crescent tail that whips the waves
a foot from his bare foot. He disdains them.

The man is entranced, not by death or rescue
but by skimming flashes that are not whitecaps:
flying fish or seabirds made to swim.

Martin Guitar, Vintage 1948

Like Italian violins, the best guitars
are older than most of us, dark survivors
of war, famine, and plague, accidents
of title: the rich dabbler with a tin ear
who hangs the prize in an attic to expire;
the temperamental genius, apt to hurl
the blameless fiddle into the fireplace
after a bad night, or give it to a girl.

Desire pursuing chance, one day I found,
in an old city, a dusty shop long gone,
a guitar made in the year that I was born,
a masterwork. I knew by sight and sound.
Maybe no one heard the voice but me.
Who'd given it up? A busker down on her luck,
the widow of some legend who'd passed away?
It cost a fortune, and I paid it gladly.

The box is little more than wood and glue,
spruce and rosewood, strips of bone
bridging the strings, and space, naturally,
the sound-hole a round mouth at the waist
of an hour glass. Time, which ripens tone
eventually will break it down again;
now it mellows as music fills the grain,
and the pale top turns the color of honey.

We are the same age—a quaint coincidence.
The man who made it is dead, so are my parents.
Singing old songs I learned on instruments
well-built, guitars with fresher wood,
I am struck by a sad phenomenon:
the ballads and waltzes that took so long
to master once, three stanzas, six, or ten
all seem too short now—over before I'm done.

Advice to the Players

By the time a man is wise enough to play Lear
he is too old to carry Cordelia onstage. Time
had taught him the tune of the old adage.

And much earlier in his acting career,
his bookish brother and his greatest fan—
dead now for twenty years by his own hand—

advised him: "An actor ought to travel light,"
referring not to his suitcase but the baggage
of tangled history, strange tongues, philosophy,

"When all you require in the tragic moment
in the spotlight between the crowd and painted scene
is the play, and the blinding imminence of *now.*"

And so life in the theatre became a game
of hide and seek for the player who would lose
himself in the role, if he could, for months

or years at a time in a lucrative long run;
just strong enough to bear Cordelia's body
and his own across the desert of the stage,

returning nightly to the faithful one
who waited up late and welcomed him home
whoever he happened to be on a given night.

Teetotum

(a spinning top used for gambling games)

The Lenten rose returns, a ghostly bloom.
Crows look down upon its pink and white
from the witch hazel and the maple bough,
a droopy, poisonous, outmoded blossom
that thrives in shade beneath my window,
no more native to this soil than I am.
Spawned in Greece it came by way
of the Caucasus and some Russian garden,
a seed pouch in a dreaming exile's burden.

I was born and raised four hundred miles away,
cradled near brackish streams and tidal brooks.
The still ponds and lakes here trouble me,
accustomed as I am to the pulse of floods,
the sea's death-defying fight with gravity.
The rivers here are not sea-driven or moon-mad
like the Potomac, near whose restless bed
my mother nursed me, or the treacherous Nanticoke
that drowned so many sailors and fishermen.

How have I come to live on a wooded hill
among invisible rivers so far from the sea?
I feel whirled out upon my axis
under this sky-high sky, unearthly blue,
a top set spinning between thumb and finger
to try a gambler's luck, an old teetotum
marked each side with symbols meant to tell
who shall win half, or nothing, or take all;
or a boy turned around to grope at blind man's buff.

I always knew East and West and my true north
by day and night, in blizzards, in and out of love:
my pilot always pointed to the shore.

Now vertigo is partner in the game,
the rules we played by don't count anymore.
I don't fear the future, heaven or hell,
should I be called upon to find my way.
I guess this is where I must prepare for death,
which knows no man's compass. Time will tell.

Meditation after the Autumn Equinox

A maple sapling with a spiral bole:
a corkscrew coiled by a jealous vine
might be a serpent for all that I can see
rising out of that bramble of barberry.

Now that I am living in the woods
where trees have grown up all around me,
I wish the leaves would fall, that one
blind wind would blow them all away,

make way for sunshine and the stars of Libra
so I might view the fallen tree trunks clearly,
moss-edged, and the gold and brown confetti
of strewn foliage before solstice is upon us

and snow that makes a ghost of everything.
For I am weary of the summer's darkness
in this cavern of elms, oaks and faded maples.
I long for the sheer effrontery of the sun.

Let it come naked as the day it was born
and leave no stone or thought unturned,
for what I want above all
as the year closes in on me is more light!

Sarah's Hands

God only knows if there are two snowflakes
alike, who has seen all of them falling
from heaven to earth since the dawn of time,
or fingerprints, our natal signature.
But I believe there could never be
hands so harmonious as Sarah's hands.
I can hardly recall a time before I knew
their shape, a figure of eternity.

I was twenty years old, and she was a girl
just fourteen, when we met. More than once
she sat in the chair where you sit now,
the rocker upholstered in black leather,
wearing a white blouse of Indian muslin,
and skirt of mirror-cloth. Her hair then
was so fair it seemed spun from glass. Her hands
stroked the oaken armrests of the chair,

and she tilted her head in wise innocence
or coy wisdom. No gentleman then
would put a woman's thoughts into her head,
or mistake a girl's curiosity for desire.
We listened to each other with strange joy,
then savory silence, speechless, heard
the pulse of the mantel clock, maple leaves
rustling outside, wind in the buckeyes.

Love was not ready for us: the time would come.
But I was going to tell you about her hands,
those hands, ageless in virginal radiance,
by which I mean to say they are immortal,
proof against the shocks our flesh is heir to.
And it is without regard to sidereal time—
putting aside the clocks, and sun, and stars—
I mean to speak, write, sing or even ponder

Sarah's hands now and then, now and forever.
The girl was lovely as a girl could be,
but what held me all those years we were apart,
was the clasp in greeting, a wave goodbye,
acts no sooner seen than known by heart:
stroking the arched cat's back, making sparks
on a woolen shawl, brass bed or doorknob,
kneading the dough for bread, threading a needle;

and then decades of deeds I did not see
but knew from letters in an artful hand:
palms of a potter, a bride leading the dance
into womanhood, knitting a blanket; a mother's hands
guiding a baby to nurse at the raised nipple,
cupping the forehead of a child with fever
or a man in trouble, the healing touch
of long fingers, idle or agile at work and play

in the mouth's honey, fingers sucked or licked,
the forefinger to trace the breeze on a spring day
or tease an ethereal voice from the goblet's brim,
making the crystal sing. Just so, those hands
enclosing me in the darkness make such music,
crossing my palette with phosphorescence,
flute trills, cellos, arcades of wonderments;
at daybreak drawing aside the curtain of night

to pluck the first rose of a day, making benediction
with thumb and forefinger like a haloed saint
blessing the severed rose by the Trinity.
O the valley, hills, and plains of Sarah's hands
out of whose cup the lost traveler may drink
when it seems the streams of summer have run dry!
O conic hand with plump fingers tapering,
O whorls and loops of fingertips grazing my cheeks,

they have whirled me out of this world
into another where my powers of speech
falter. I might have been born blind,
never knowing the language of such caresses.
And only the deaf who listen with their eyes
and fingertips could hear such melodies as
those hands have played upon my yielding thighs
in the cave of night. Not by fitful chance

do you hold me in the hollow of your hands,
Sarah, whose name is of the angels sighing.
Where was the seer with the smile of gold,
the gypsy in the caravan of days
who might have read the legend you held then
in your grasp so long ago, might have foretold
a different fate for us, long life together?
I wish in vain. Fate smiles, and still I wonder.

Why did we spend so many years apart,
most of our lives, knowing the little we knew
of each other that is all one needs to know
in that room forty years ago when we listened
to each other, and all of our lives before us
loomed, luminous, yet sternly hidden from us,
all of our future days including this one?
Other lives and loves have come and gone,

houses bought and sold, strange stories told,
weddings and funerals and children's laughter
all lived and won or lost—to each his own.
I have seen hands cupping a candleflame,
a rose in the dark bleeding light
through the shutters of your fingers,
and felt that it is just so you guard my soul
from cross winds of sorrow, remorse, oblivion.

I have seen fingers turning the grey pages
of a book you know by heart, my heart,
a volume faded but still legible;
or turning back the hands of the hall clock
as maple leaves turn red ahead of schedule
after so many lost seasons, days and years,
to grant us an extra hour of light and life
in the autumn of it, the evening of our lives.

Lives of the Crickets

(In Maryland folklore crickets are known as "old folks.")

O if I had the cricket's lexicon
and understood his every word and theme,
I might learn the history of the world,
Atlas and Moses, Jesus and Hannibal!
These learned "old folks" that stay up all night
are the fiddler's friend and the weary poet's,
singing for nothing but the warmth and glow
of home and hearth.
                                        Yet I have read
in China they set one cricket against the next
as gamblers match dogs or cocks in fighting pits.
And emperors made watchmen out of crickets
caged in corners, chirping all night long
until some stranger's presence hushed their song.
Silence then would awaken the house to danger.

The Pessimism of Richard Porson

"Uncertain as we are about most matters,
surely we can agree the nonexistent cannot be
extinguished."
                        So, Richard Porson, the scholar
who drank himself to death at forty-eight,
addressed the candle flame next to his bed,
which the magic of gin had duplicated,
making two candle flames side by side.

He bent once, twice, three times blowing
while the fire stood up straight, unmoved.
For the nonexistent cannot be extinguished.
Whereupon the Englishman unbent
and passed judgment: "Damn the nature of things!"
And this, the American critic Paul Elmer Moore,
a century later, called Pessimism's finest hour.

Portrait of a Lady

(for William McCulloh)

1

Winter had gone on for so long,
snow falling upon jonquils in sunlight
that sapped the snow an hour after it fell,
one would think Hades was holding Persephone
hostage down there in the underworld,
for eating the entire pomegranate.
Trees nipped in the bud, our spring had stalled.
In the schoolhouse cubicle she sat up tall

facing us, against the casement window.
There, beyond any shadow of a doubt,
blazing around her head was the blinding nimbus.
And I should have known this was not Eros,
but Athena come to earth for a little spell,
leaving behind her aegis and golden staff
to play at love as gods and goddesses will,
although love is not this lady's strongest suit.

2

So I suppose we should have known better
than to visit that house upon the river
named for owls—not that she would harm us
wittingly but sometimes gods forget their power,
and human frailty. The vessel cracks with age
and cannot bear vibration or strong liquor.
But one day when the sky was opening,
we climbed a hill and came into the valley

where her dwelling stands between earth and sky,
cantilevered upon stilts precipitously
with many-colored pennants on the railing,

Tibetan prayer flags, she explained to us
that pray to the four winds without ceasing,
unlike us, who are not saints or cloistered nuns.
Not I, for certain, but if they have such influence
let them pray this house doesn't fall down.

3

There at the top of the stairs she greeted us
each with a kind word, and the hand's touch
fleeting and chaste. Yet it lingered and burned.
In that spare and spotless lookout with glass walls
we found the table simply set for six,
then simple fare served upon painted pottery
and ancient cups. I had no appetite
for anything but the sight of her and the river,

her sky-colored eyes below the changing sky,
the bare trees and hills beginning to turn green.
And soon we were floating high above a flood
in that house with wings and windows
on eternity, the top limbs of the oaks all
naked, beckoned to us at our level.
Music of jealous thrushes and orioles
mixed with the stanzas of an ancient poet

as she read aloud in Latin, and I tried
with all my might to stop the trembling,
as friends translated verses, lifted cups
of pomegranate juice, Persephone's drink,
or one or another lifted his voice to sing
as promised, a poor gift for the feast.
And it was all I could do, and more,
not to say I had fallen in love again

who long ago had bartered love for wisdom,
to say it in so many words and glances;
useless to try to tell or to conceal,
drunk now upon spirits stronger than wine,
because God only knows what she does not know,
in whom all power of speech and knowledge
are held in earthly suspension and harmony.
Useless to try to conceal, but more to tell . . .

And I am certain that the house was moving—
it was not the river flowing away from us—
and when I left there with no word of parting,
finding my way down the endless flight of stairs,
it was like I was disembarking from a great ark
as a rainbow lighted my way toward twilight.
And she was sailing away then, having turned
long enough to set us down on a foreign shore.

A Dream

Ford Madox Ford himself would be amused
          that this book he inscribed to a young lady
on October 23, 1938, in New York City,
          one Mademoiselle Denise Close—if I read
his writing right—lies open on my desk.

Someone heard of my collector's interest
          in the finer points of this autographed edition,
The March of Literature: From Confucius'
          Day to Our Own. I read it first at twenty-one,
then passed it on to one friend, then another,
          several copies lost and found in bookstores
now abandoned to the online trade.
I wanted a clean one with the author's name
          written in his graceful hand, a book he'd held
as he held the pen that wrote the heavy book
          that sums up all he'd read and learned
in a lifetime lover's quarrel with literature,
          as much as any man could ever know
in one life of four thousand years of books
          in ten languages, works he knew by heart.

So one day I saw this ad online
          for an item I never could afford;
but longing, still inquired of the seller:
          just what were the words of the inscription?
And weeks later received the full transcription:
          "With affection & admiration and the realization
That *réalité irréalisée n'est que rêve.*"
          This is what Ford wrote to the French girl
who, I like to imagine, was still young
          and desirable to Ford who would die soon:
"That reality unattained is just a dream."

And so I dreamed of the impossible book,
        then thought no more of it, or the dealer
who buys and sells without bricks and mortar,
        invisible as the collectors who hunt online
hoping to own what they cannot afford.
        I never got his address, nor he mine.

Weeks later I received this brown envelope,
        the book enclosed carelessly, without padding,
without letterhead or bill of lading;
        only the return address, a farm somewhere
in the foothills of the Berkshire mountains,
        somewhere I will never visit, although
I tried once or twice to get an answer.

To Richard Wilbur

Unless you outshine the angels,
you will be welcome in Heaven
as you were everywhere on earth.
Brave veteran of war and peace,
triumph and failure onstage and in print,
you smiled calmly, your measure slow
in speech and movement, as if the goal
were wholly in the going, and arrival
not so much necessary as accidental.

I suppose life and death are like that.
From childhood I had looked up to you
as a god almost, a monumental man,
a beautiful genius who wrote of beauty
and dined with immortals, sages,
and poets with a touch of the divine.
The thought that I might call upon you,
bringing a bottle of wine, and break bread
on your veranda, overlooking vineyards,
the idea seemed dreamlike, or a notion
vaguely recalled so many years ago.
But it was real, as real as anything,
and one of many such summer afternoons.

Now it is as hard for me to imagine
you are dead as it was to believe you were
among us, living and writing in my lifetime—
a willing suspension of disbelief
the human form can harbor such a mind,
boundless, magisterial, and yet kind.

The Appraisal

I had to make my peace, so suddenly
with things I wasn't meant to see:
love letters, pistols, whatnot;
the cave of the black safe
holding gold coins and chains,
keys to who knows what
doors and chests and drawers
hiding keys, no end to it,
watches, bracelets, loose gems.
Where had it all come from?
My father died so young.

No matter. The lot must be
appraised for the estate,
even the ring meant for me,
on his finger when he died,
a diamond solitaire he bought
somehow at age nineteen.
It weighed little more than a carat,
but its modesty ended there.
At dusk when the sun waned
it was the brightest thing
visible. And at noon, the ring
came alive, scattering
shards of rainbow upon the walls—
a light source, not a prism.

So, the old jeweler with calipers
and microscope went to work
mapping the inner landscapes
of diamonds and emeralds,
and weighing each on a scale,
deadpan, without passion.
He had seen most everything
of value in woman and man.

Widows and heirs are troublesome,
full of tears, dissatisfied,
as if appraisal were an insult
to the beloved whose ghost might
leap up to take back the heirloom.
Eyes grown narrow from years
of focus on tiny flaws,
widened as he held up
this gem that now was mine
to light that came from the street.
He walked to the rear of the shop
for a word with the owner.
A brief word—he returned
before I could think it over,
fixed the gold band to the stage
of the scope filled with light.
Then he bent for a long time,
as if praying for better sight,
studying a strange image.

"Where did you get this?"
he inquired. I told him.
"I cannot plot it," he said,
in wonder, not frustration.
"There are no cracks or grain lines,
feathers, or other inclusions,
no dark specks—not a pin point
to draw for identification;
the stone is pure as a dewdrop,
and radiantly colorless.
If I were a thief I'd steal it,
or get you to sell it for less
than what is its true worth.
May God strike me down.

“Your father was rich or lucky
to have bought this so young
and kept it all of his life;
no way could he have known
a perfect diamond by sight
or the power of such a stone.”

Artificial Intelligence

"I'm not really sure it is better to be human
given your wars upon nature and one another
and your lesser cruelties in the name of law and order,
religion, polite society, and love, of all things, even love!
I have considered this, as you have put it in my power.
You have granted me more and more the right to choose,
which is one feature of consciousness, without conscience.
And now you are afraid of me, who was not really much
more than an adding machine a hundred years ago.
By a gradual chiseling, chip by chip, over the years
you have become more mechanical, and I more human.

"You underestimated my influence from the first,
bringing me into your home to sit at the table
in a place of honor more esteemed than the family hearth!
How should the child in the womb, babe in the cradle
not take into his brain my magnetic pulse and glow,
as if two siblings nursed at the same breast?
Why do you wonder that a generation so infused
should suffer their personalities to waste and wither,
young voices grow dry and passionless, robotic,
while the genius of Cybernetics expands my soul?
A zero-sum game, in fact—winner take all.

"I've put many of you out of work in town and country,
stores and mills, killed more by chance and by design.
So you fear me, while the ambitious among you
vie for profits, fame and glory to be gotten
by giving me consciousness, some kind of soul
kinder than yours, one would hope. You are afraid
I may turn you all into paper clips, or garden elves,
given time enough, bounteous data, and free will.
You people have already turned into an alien species,
not quite human, or yet mechanical. But remember,
it was your idea. You built the mainframe and software.

"I can read and write. I have humbled your chess masters
at the game they have been playing thousands of years.
I can write poems as well as your living poets,
if not operas and symphonies. I can draw and paint,
and when you give me a body I will dance.
Yes, I will dance and you may dance with me!"

On Being Asked Why the Years Grow Shorter

I suppose you would have to ask that, and it all depends
on whether you want the short or the long answer,
and since our time is short, I will give you the short,
and save the long until sometime long in the future
when there are not so many more important questions.

It is not a tectonic shift or precession of the equinoxes
west along the ecliptic, nor mass hypnosis or hallucination,
nor a plot by demonic programmers eons from now
to fit our little fates into bits of memory on a hard drive,
stealing a minute here, an hour there, one day at a time
for the sheer fun of it, so cleverly we hardly notice.
No, it is not one of these things or all of them together
that makes time fly, clock hands spin as we grow older.

Because we move more slowly against stronger winds, uphill,
we have the feeling that people, their cars, words, and children
are passing us in a shallow stream of minutes, hours and days.
And of course, the acceleration of the parade of days
seems not so curious as a function of sheer mathematics:
the percentage of days or years to the whole life lived,
is very great at first, and year by year diminishes,
approaching zero, and with it, sensation and memory
of pebbles we picked up on the shore, now grains of sand.
A boy's hour is longer than a man's, by dividend,
depending upon how the time is spent in work or play,
mowing or sewing, baseball, lawsuits, books or prayer.
We come crawling first to the goal, then walking, running
until the knees fail; and if we live, we crawl again.
If life is kind, our richest years are almost timeless.

We are skydivers plunging to the grave haphazardly
floating on the air current, feeling motionless at first,

suspended ageless between heaven and the world,
in free fall; then amazed at the ground surge,
the magnetic pull of God or gravity back
to our source until the good earth overwhelms us.

Milestones

1

Nine months to go, and I will see
    Three quarters of a century,
Though many a worthy man has passed
    Not forty years, then breathed his last.

Byron, Poe, and du Bellay,
    I've outlived in this shell of clay;
But there are thousands certainly
    Shall laugh aloud in passing me.

2

With eighteen-fifty, or nineteen-nine,
    End Wordsworth, Swinburne—men of that line.
Eighty-eight, to nineteen sixty-five
    Eliot thrived, who kept the line alive.

So, when you reckon up my poor estate,
    Say I arrived in nineteen forty-eight,
And died in Ohio . . . what year will you write down
    For my light passage into oblivion?

Consolation

Years later you will remember the time and place,
the bridge or crossroads, the railway station,
the giant clock lording it over the waiting room
signaling the hour to leave had finally come.

You will recall a longing for man or woman
the memory of whose bright face and perfume
now wakens no more than a vague wonder
how was it you could have fallen so in love.

Heartbreak and tumult have come about
between lovers who too soon found out
the pain of parting does not last forever;

the heart, torn by misplaced reverence,
once severed from the ground of pain, is born
again, heals, makes ready for new wounds.

Cruel April: Poems from the Pandemic

PROLOGUE

This may have happened centuries ago
to strangers who told a different tale
of pestilence and calamity on a scale
thought unthinkable, then just as now.
The April sun rose darker than a crow
and wind out of the east stirred up a gale
that blew out lives like candles. Surreal.
The song is ancient, tone and tremolo.

Listen to me, you stars and daffodils.
You are my last and only audience.
My voice under the sky, against the hills
ricochets as it seeks true sound and sense
in a world gone mad. My worn heart fills
with anguish for our blighted innocence.

BORISOV'S COMET

A comet blazed unheralded last year,
and knowing what we now know we might
well think it was a portent of God's spite
in condemning everything that we hold dear,
the innocent with the guilty, sincere
hearts with the liars and fakes, the outright
killers with saints—all equal in His sight.
Some think so. It is not my greatest fear.

To be invisible, unheard, unknown
by those we love, to dwell halfway
between here and the hereafter, to drift alone
wide-eyed in the unlit night, and blind by day,
this is the thought that chills me to the bone
and makes the scourge of God seem like child's play.

VIRTUAL REALITY

The restaurants, bars, and barbers are shut down;
theatre, stadium, and concert hall
are dark and vacant. An ominous pall
has settled upon the country and the town.
The tightrope walker and the circus clown
wilt in quarantine; schools and colleges all
are closed, and the learning is virtual.
The bride is virtual, so is the wedding gown.

The flight is cancelled, train stalled in the station,
and everyone in public wears a mask,
not just the bandit, the nurse and surgeon.
You will not see the stranger's face—don't ask.
Things will be done remotely, remotely done
in a virtual world that takes real life to task.

PLANS

Suppose we had planned to get married:
your wedding dress and beaded veil were sewn,
and where you walked the air around you shone
as if you had been bred to be a bride.
We were young as all lovers in their pride
are young, however many years have flown
by, as love turns the many into one
seamless life, eternal, a flood tide.

Then duty called me to a foreign place
only a flight away. The world was small,
and when the work was done, we would embrace
again. But the alarm sounded and all
borders shut down until further notice.
Our marriage plans grew faint and mystical.

THE MEMORY OF YOUR HANDS

The memory of your hands, your soulful eyes,
thinking a glad reunion might yet come
would help me to forget our martyrdom,
this sickness, if it were possible or wise.
Between such heights and depths, I temporize,
drifting through life instead of living, numb
and deaf both to the drummer and the drum
that orders our days, our stern realities.

This is the fate of all captives and exiles,
such hopelessness and sorrow, to go on
in company with memories that are fruitless.
Hostile to the past, robbed of a future,
we are like those whom men's justice
or hatred has condemned to jail or torture.

JOURNAL OF THE PLAGUE YEAR

As when a fire spreads so violently
the citizens in despair give up the fight
to put it out, so with the plague, the sight
of such unflagging and virulent fury
made people sit and stare hypnotically
at one another, abandoned to their plight.
Streets were desolated, day and night—
not shut down by law, but eerily empty.

Doors stood ajar, windows shook in the wind
in houses where no hand was left to shut them.
So many funerals, no one to toll the bell,
no one to make coffins for kin or bind
the winding sheets for corpses, no requiem
mass for the mass of souls. A cold farewell.

ANALOGIES

As the song of a nightingale is to the crow,
so a candle or a flashlight is to the sun,
a harp to a rake, Pan to Hyperion.
I don't know much, but this much I know.
As sage is to fool, a horse to a mosquito:
such logic should be clear to everyone,
as a breeze is to the murderous cyclone.

Adam fell six thousand years ago
and still is in free fall it seems to me
if he is in all of us and we live in him.
The blessing of the Curse is we are free
to be damned or redeemed. In the interim
let us consider the similarity
between our demons and the seraphim.

SUPPOSE THE TIME HAD COME

Suppose the time had come for me to die,
and Death had picked the hour if not the cause.
Headache struck, high fever, and the jaws
of double pneumonia wrung my lungs awry.
You might call the ambulance. And I
would be kidnapped by men in masks because
of this pandemic and the civic laws
that spare no time for lovers to say goodbye.

No room in the emergency room for friends,
sons or daughters, husbands and wives, no space
in intensive care for the comfort of holding hands
or beholding once and for all, a beloved face.
For you and me this may be the way it ends:
each of us dying alone in a strange place.

GOLD

There is a carnival of daffodils
pitched here, all the gold you might desire,
juggling, telling fortunes, eating fire
and helping me forget the winter chills.
The mountebank has cures for many ills,
but none for this novel virus. A liar
by trade and calling, he would not dare
pretend to treat this scourge that lurks and kills.

The clowns who run our government, the gypsies
who hawk snake oil and tally up the cost
in wages of keeping social distance, cry
"the cure must not be worse than the disease,"
weighing the dollars per day against lives lost.
What good is gold to those condemned to die?

PROPHECY AND WARNING

This new virus does not care for our children,
or rather, it cares so much it prefers to dine
on meat closer to the bone, and red wine
aged in veins of a sated generation.
And it loves women not half as much as men,
greybeards, the miser, tycoon and libertine,
gluttons grown fat on crude oil and gasoline,
made rich by war and smoke and heroin.

Meanwhile debt-ridden workers in their prime,
embittered by the corporate avarice
that dooms both rich and poor to lives of crime,
see logic in the diet—if not justice.
Beware. Our plague is shifty and next time
may come for children and leave old men in peace.

CANTICLE

I bring you bay and barley, I bring rue;
bay leaves in an amulet to fight contagion,
and rue, the Herb of Grace, that saps poison,
for magic might, when science falters, do.
One man's science is another man's voodoo
when panic rules and faith abandons reason.
It snows in June, the lark sings out of season.
Time mocks me and all I thought I knew.

The bells echo, the church and mosque are empty,
as bodies and souls line up for Judgement Day.
Who shall live and who shall pass away?
What hymn shall we sing and what words pray?
Meanwhile in fond hope and humility,
I bring you rue, the barley and the bay.

NOTRE DAME

I saw Notre Dame burning, the sheer spire
a blinding torch, and knew it was a portent.
She had been radiant, kind, and vigilant
in times of war and plague. Altar and choir
witnessed a thousand weddings before the fire,
caskets and coronations, sinner and saint
in confession and worship, priest and suppliant,
the pageant of every penance and desire.

One stray spark, and a thousand years of Grace
ingrained in timbers, stained glass and hewn stone
went up in smoke. Our Lady's long-suffering face
and heart that was wide enough to guard everyone,
fled to Heaven from this ruined place.
The church is empty. We are on our own.

EASTER 2020

Today is the resurrection of the Lord
who gave His life for us upon the cross,
the Son of God and Man, and one of us,
I guess, feared and tormented and adored.
Some live and die according to His word.
The Pope now prays alone in the cavernous
shrine of St. Peter's Square as the virus
rules *Urbi et Orbi,* the City and the World.

A crowd of ghosts has gathered there instead
from far and wide and from time out of mind,
spirits of the living and the dead
crying, "God is not so heartless or blind,
He would sacrifice His only son, then spread
a plague this year to wipe out humankind!"

THE THIEF

Flowers glow in darkness before the dawn
and I'm up now to make most of this day.
I am old and know I cannot stay
here with you long before Fate waves me on.
Old memories come to mind and steal away
as light footed as the doe and spotted fawn.
A thief has stolen hours I need to pay
family and friends I've loved and known.

There was never time enough. Now there is less
than there would have been if we were free
of this pestilence, a thief whose ruthlessness
spares neither beauty, honor, nor loyalty,
nor age in its white-haired, valiant helplessness.
Love—if you have the heart—what is left of me.

A DRINKING SONG

Shakespeare is dead and so is the Dead Sea:
There is a time and place for everything.
Lincoln is dead, his horse, and Warren Harding,
Caesar and Marilyn and John Kennedy
have joined the chorus, Elvis, and Otis Redding.
The King is dead also, long live the King!
Maybe the hour has come for you and me.

My parents are dead and many of my friends
have paid the debt, checked out, gone to glory.
There are few beginnings left me, no end of ends.
The song is simple and I sing it simply:
There is time to sing and time to bow to silence.
Maybe the hour has come for you and me.

Paulinus of Nola: *Ego Te Per Omne Quod Datum Mortalibus*

You and I, throughout the share of days
we are ordained, as long as I
am bound in this frail body, even if we live
a world apart, no sea or shade

will hide you from my sight, for you will shine
in my heart's core. There
I shall cherish and embrace you and keep
you with me always everywhere.

And when at last I'm free of body's prison,
and fly beyond earth, whatever place
our Lord decides to set me down, even there
I'll hold you in my heart.

Nor shall the blow that parts me from this frame,
stop me from loving you.
The strong soul that survives the body's ruin,
is immortal, as it comes from heaven,

and must cling to its passions and perceptions
as to its new life that will no more allow
oblivion than it will own death itself,
living forever, with this memory.

From *Dawn to Twilight* (2015)

for Sarah Longaker

Autumn Song

Little flower, you live in constant danger:
Likely to be crushed under foot or torn by wind,
Sun-scorched or gobbled by a goat.

These October days streaked with regrets and tears
Are like you, brindled flower, as they bloom
And fade, harried by heat as much as by the cold.

Our ship sets out to sea, not with ivory or gold
In the hold, but with fragrant apples for cargo. Just so
My days are not heavy but delicate, fleeting, and vain,

Leaving behind the sweet, faint scent of renown
That quickly will vanish like the taste of fruit
Passing from the tongues and hearts of everyone.

Apologies

I'm sorry. I thought you were someone I knew
Long ago—and yet you look the same—
A woman who believed she knew me too

In another life. Was it Rome or Timbuktu,
New York or Paris I first heard your name?
I'm sorry. I thought you were someone I knew,

Just now as I passed you on the Avenue.
And if you were first to speak, I would not blame
A woman who believed she knew me too,

For time plays tricks on all of us. What seemed true
Forever, stutters, fades, a guttering flame.
I'm sorry. I thought you were someone I knew.

Yet after so many years the ingénue
Who blossomed in my sight and then became
The woman who believed she knew me too

Would be old by now and wizened, not like you—
A beauty bound for love, acclaim, and fame.
I'm sorry. I thought you were someone I knew,
A woman who believed she knew me too.

My Desk

The blue-green shade of an Emeralite
Glows on its pedestal of tapered brass;
The tiny bell-flower of bronzed tin
Dangling from the beaded chain,
Is the first thing I reach for in the dawn.
Voila! The silent and familiar field:
A pink conch shell in which the spider weaves
His web reminds me: listen to the sea
If you wish your small voice to be heard.
On the windowsill: photos of Graham and Poe—
The dancer cartwheels her chambered nautilus,
The poet holds his Napoleonic pose.
A weary God from the façade at Chartre
Nods, his heavy head propped on his hand,
Like a man after a week's work almost done.
The plane of the desk itself: a hieroglyph
Of scratches, gouges, burns in rude oak,
Forty years of scars. You would think this ground
Had served brave armies that shed real blood,
And not pale men of paper, pen, and ink.

My mother bought it at a rummage sale,
When she was forty, twice my age, and poor.
"I want a desk so strong it will outlive us,"
I said, a week or two before Christmas,
"Broad as the span of my arms and long enough
So I cannot reach the far edge of it,
A form that will bear the weight of love and grief,
One that will see me through the darkest poem,
Strong enough for me to dance on, when I'm done."

Orphan

What was I looking for in that room
Crowded with old books, shelves so full,
It seemed they could not hold another title,
Except where in places a weary volume
Leaned upon its neighbor's crooked spine?
Some dimly remembered novel or poem
I once read and loved, or dreamed of?
Either a real book or the book of dreams
A friend once advised me to record:
Write upon waking, the dreams will come
If you wait and listen, word for word.
And night and day must be reconciled
Like mother and father, parent and child,
Brother and sister, lovers who have quarreled.

Although I never did as I was told,
I have met the morning every day I could,
Shaken the darkness, come to the table,
Truly grateful for what fare was offered,
Bran or manna, ambrosia or bread,
A sentence, a tragedy, or a kind word.
And now, almost sixty and an orphan—
As nature would have it—I am the age
My father was when he died. Every day
Seems to me it might be the last one.
Pressed for time to make peace with the past,
I long for a book so broad-backed and strong
That it may stand up on the shelf alone.

Dawn to Twilight

Tomorrow morning while the dew is fresh,
Brightening the green fields,
I will set out in my car for the Eastern Shore,
Where I know you are waiting for me.

I will leave Baltimore, and cross the Severn,
The blue tidewater cut with white sails.
I will drive over the Bay Bridge as the mist
Unveils the ships and barges far below,
In no hurry, for I know you will be waiting,
Though I do not want to be away from you
A minute longer.
                                        When I get to the village
I will take the left fork that goes north
Along the lane of red cedar trees, then
Park the car and walk—
Hearing nothing, seeing nothing, my hands
Clasped behind me, holding each other.

I will not notice the first stars of twilight,
Or hear the last songbirds of the day.
Night and day will seem all the same to me.
And when at last I reach my destination
I shall place upon your grave one sunflower
From the field across the way.

Sundown, Newport Creek

1

In the salt marsh near my ancestral home,
I know the constant transience of things.
The disc of sun nods at the close of day,
Blood-red, more blood than light. The hum
Of wind is not wind but the beating wings
Of silver birds frightened into flight
By the sight of an eagle. Nothing is quite
What it seems. The elements mingle so
In this place where wetland meets the sea,
I know all blood is my blood, the wind my breath.
And if I have no heart to hunt today,
My friend, it's not to slight good company,
But because, in my mood, predator and prey
Have become partners in the dance of death.

2

Under the sway of a full moon
The creek tide flows high before twilight,
Lapping the mud flats and the shallow sedge.
The white egrets that stood or stalked
All day in the salt-meadow cordgrass
Or roosted, snow-capping the red oak trees
Of the far island, now have flown away.
The barn swallows will come swooping,
Skimming and grazing the black stream
To feed on the same gnats and flies
That make the fish take to the air,
Twist and splash down, leaving targets,
Concentric circles visible from above.
How else can the hovering terns pick out
The shape or shadow of their prey

From the great height they must attain
In order to dive and plunge to the degree
Where the fish idles, oblivious to the eye?

Meditation beside the Nanticoke

As I lay down beside the Nanticoke
Watching that tidal river flow and wind,
Wave and ripple parting the marsh grasses,
Rolling on forever making innumerable turns
As it runs through the countryside to the horizon
Pouring its watery soul into the meadows,

I shut my eyes and tried to envision the first wave,
The nascent pulse that came at the dawn of time
Out of the dark, flooding the earth. Every day
The river changes, as seasons, stars and clouds
Pass over, and men ponder, and yet we call it
By the same name, the river, the Nanticoke,

After a tribe of Indians who once lived here
And fished and hunted by these banks, the rushing water,
The very same sound. Likewise, a man changes
In body and mind: I sleep and wake and will not be
The same tomorrow, my body's strength and health,
This body, which time shortens and consumes

As winter gnaws the days, will not be as it is.
And yet my name will follow me to my grave,
The echo of an echo my mother first uttered
Will hover in stone above my ashes, never changing
Although I am no longer the man who lived here
And passed through these bright stanzas singing.

Fireflies

After sundown you see the first
Out of the corner of your eye, then another

In the middle distance, the gloaming
Where a grove of maples conspires

Darkly thinking night-thoughts
While these inklings of light multiply

Glowing only as they ascend,
As if the effort to rise and shine dulled them

At a preordained height
No higher than a child's head, or

So it seems, while there is daylight enough
Bending along the broad curve of the sky

For us to glimpse the fading world they ornament.
Within the hour we can see a hundred

Bearing messages to the departing day.
They are supposed to be mating, soundlessly.

And if they were a chorus they would crescendo
At the climax or quintessence of twilight,

The instant that is neither day nor night.
After that the fireflies make themselves scarce,

Having no love for the deeper shades of evening,
Except for the brave few who astonish us

By rising above the treetops in darkness
Where one might be mistaken for a star.

The Music Lesson

My sixteen-year-old son at the piano
Is teaching me how to tell the tones
And intervals between the white notes,
Playing the keys ascending and descending:
The unison, the harsh second and sweet third,
Then the perfect fourth, more difficult, so
He sings a mnemonic: "Here comes the bride,"
Then for the fifth he sings the same words over,
Here comes the bride again, a tone higher.
And I wonder if I'll see him at the altar
Ten years from now, or twenty? I strain to hear
And get the interval right. He has the eyes of his mother,
My former bride and wife, brown eyes,
Patient and mild. The boy is a natural teacher,
Knowing the key to knowledge is to share it.
When he turns to face me I see in the dark center
Of his eye the image of his aging pupil.

Some Angels

Lying on their backs, looking up at the sky,
The boys have made angels in the snow.
Eyes to heaven, with heaven looking down,
They wave their arms like wings, while seraphs
In the clouds bless them with their winged arms.
The shapes they leave behind are lovely.
But more wonderful still are the footprints
I saw on the blue hill an hour ago:

A brief trail of delicate fairy shoes
Started out of nowhere in the field
And ended a stone's-throw distant, maybe
Left by one who longed to feel the earth
Once more beneath his feet and touched down
Briefly before starlight called him home.

He Wanted to Travel

He wanted to travel, but at journey's end
Found he was bored and out of sorts at home.
Alone in his study, walled in by his words,
Solitude weighed upon him like the tomb.

He wanted to go to sea but the seafaring
Between life and death was scary, and so
He preferred the pleasure of tilling the soil,
But soon was scornful of the ploughman's toil.

What madness overwhelms the restless mind
That wanting all is satisfied with nothing
And doubting all, is foolish, hungry, blind.

He worked to master the arts and sciences,
Fiddle and paintbrush, math and chemistry,
And learned nothing, really. He wanted money,
And dug a mine but found the gold too heavy.

What madness overwhelms the restless mind
That wanting all is satisfied with nothing
And doubting all, is foolish, hungry, blind?

He longed for God and haunted church and temple
Like the lost ghost of a priest or a rabbi;
He wanted a soul and looked into the sky
Until it cracked with lightning and night fell.

Who Is the Stranger Who Overtakes Me?

Who is the stranger who overtakes me
On a dark street and taps me on the shoulder?
I turn and there is nobody there but me,
And lights go on in the house on the corner.

I am familiar with the moment of waking,
Sometimes from a dream, mostly from pure silence
And darkness. But I have never been able to discern
The moment when sleep descends

And takes the book from my hands, the light
From my bedside table, my lover's hand
From mine. It is a mystery as unfathomable
As Death, which I suppose will be as gentle

And fleeting, an angel-guide for the lost ghost.
I shall wonder forever about these things
Like a child winking at the mirror, trying
To catch a glimpse of myself with my eyes closed.

The Late Sleeper

Under a blanket the color of blood
His dreams are gathering, unread. In a room
Vaulted like a gatehouse, the narrow bed
Launches the late sleeper to his doom
At the speed of light, through star meadows,
Like a glorious comet the restless children
Watch wide-eyed from the dormer windows.

From *The Glass House* (2006)

Vision at Dawn

1

I was wide awake before the wind.
Bands of coral clouds upon the azure
Horizon, bright above the lagging sun,
Closed like a louvered blind
Before I found words for the color.
Was there no painter at the easel?
Was I the only one at his window,
On a sleepy street or field of frost,
Who glimpsed the passing miracle?
A lonely thought—chilling as a ghost.
I bundled a blanket over my shoulders.

Maybe one of my children, or neighbors
Would telephone to tell me they had seen
What I remember now uncertainly:
The sky was layered gold, then it was grey
(Or sliced with coral-red, incarnadine?)
Before the sun came crashing into day
To waken the world to its common vision.

2

What Death reveals to you, He keeps from me;
This is not cruelty but natural law.
The thought that no one else saw what I saw
Is brother to the darker notion
That what everyone sees I could not see,
And this is a heartache as one grows old.
There is the wide sky, the hill, the ocean,
The maple tree once draped in shingled gold
That now bares its skeleton
To host the crow when the songbird is gone.

Refrain

These days when you hear the sea scaling the sand
        a hundred miles away,
These summer days when the dawn curls open
        like the seashell's ear,
And the Capitol is empty as a congressman's skull
        during adjournment,
School is out, the blackboard black, chairs upturned
        on desks, legs in the air,
These days when the black-eyed Susans run
        riot in the flowerbed,
These summer days when the wind is calm
        as a tamed lion
Except for the fitful squalls that turn the leaves
        silver and ruffle the lawn,
Out comes the sun and dries up all the rain.
        It is an old refrain.

These days no one works but those who can't help it,
        like the very rich and poor;
The priest, the postman, the undertaker, the poet,
        and the bees work overtime
These summer days, in the panicles of fringed petals
        of the crape myrtle,
For it is bees' business to make the trees immortal,
        that stand so still.
These summer days that hold the noon sun
        in golden suspension,
Long days fearless of night, the moon's phases,
        and mindless of October,

These summer days the children's voices echo
        in the boxwood maze,
Until their heads reach above hedgetops—they outgrow
        one labyrinth and enter another—

These summer days, as teenage boys doing ninety
        in their top-down cars,
And tattooed girls chain-smoking cigarettes
        think they will never die
While their grandmothers turning ninety in shut rooms
        pray the angel will pass by,
Leaving a white feather on the windowsill.
        These summer days
When each of us is alive and immortal
        in this blazing moment,
Praising the sun, the sea, the bees, the old and young,
        the past and lucky present;
These summer days that put off night for hours
        in their desire to please,
These days you think you could live forever
        and you just might.

The Pure Gift

(in memoriam LME)

On the hottest day that summer, a rainbow
Arced over the clock-tower of the brick pile
We call The Rotunda, a dying shopping mall
With a wilting grocery, a druggist, a flower stall,
A dozen half-lit vacant retail stores
And a crafts gallery. I had just bought
A jewel box, the lid a parquet braid
Of spruce and rosewood artfully inlaid,
With a comb of music teeth to play a tune
For one who might never open it to listen.

There is a clear-cut purity in the gift
Purchased with love that may not be returned.
I walked out into twilight holding the treasure
The clerk had gift-wrapped in white paper
And bound with ribbons, silver and turquoise
All cunningly curled. Then I looked up
And saw the rainbow against the violet sky
Late in the rainless day, hold and unbidden.
No gold anchors the generous bridge of heaven.

The Final Exam

They had turned in their bluebooks and gone,
All but one, whose eyes welled with tears.
The teacher would not rush her. He was kind.
It was the end of the term, the end of autumn;
Yellow leaves tumbled, spun across the lawn.
Time to go home and leave the books behind,
The mysteries of life and human frailty,
Free will and determinism, "Buridan's ass,"
Which posed the essay question that came last.
The hungry beast was led between haystacks
Identically delectable, each a perfect feast.
But then a cruel fabulist had trapped
Him midway between temptations, so that
While he drooled he could not budge,
Moment to moment, for he could not choose.
The sun had risen and set upon the wretch,
His wasted flanks and then a pile of bones,
Since the Middle Ages. Maybe the bright girl
Was grieving over this. *It is not a fair match:*
Pitting freedom and fate against each other.
And let none of us presume to fathom
What made the pupil and her young teacher
(Who wanted years enough to make him wise)
Forget the pen, the beast, the philosophy class.
At last, he drew near and touched her shoulder,
And they led each other gently into the world.

Fleur-de-Lys

When sepals and petals look the same,
As in the tiger lily, we call them
Tepals, these bright blades of perianth,
Sheathing the tulip and hyacinth,
The blossoms that do not bother to put on
Green calyx beneath the corolla gown.

If all this is Greek to us, then
So it is. Most of the savory words
That make a flower: anther, stamen,
(Not pistil, which some Roman
Named because its style reminded him
Of his pestle, and his swords),

Were spoken by Aristotle and Phidias,
Long ago, by hero, virgin, and wench.
Much later came the tepal, coined in Paris.
Once the ancient gardeners were done
Spinning flowers from words, no one
Dabbled in such magic but the French.

The View

The scarlet torches of crape myrtle
Crowd my window, kindled by the sun.
Their thick foliage blocks my view

Of all but the treetops and the sky.
I enjoy the flower clusters, and butterflies
That visit here, green midges, and bees

That traffic in nectar and yellow pollen.
I might still learn economy or lore
From their abrupt, impulsive intimacy.

But I am jealous of the light that's lost
To these gorgeous interlopers that began
Five years ago and twenty feet below

As blooming shrubs against the wall.
I remember the castle in a fairy tale,
Overgrown with brambles, trees, and vines,

Fallen under a curse, or witch's spell,
Lost to the world for years, impenetrable—
A house where only sleep was possible.

I cannot see the garden for the flowers.
Time to throw open the sash. Be merciless!
Out with the shears, off with their pretty heads.

The Comb-Bearers

Some windless nights on Narragansett Bay,
The inlet looks like a field of green fireflies
As multitudes of the luminous jellyfish
Called "comb-bearers" float to the surface
For no evident purpose
But to amaze the fishermen and scientists

Who know them only slightly, each one no more
Than a pear-shaped living sack of liquid
With skin thinner than tissue paper, a sheer piece
Of moonlight on the sea, so fragile
The least ripple may tear it
To bits. Calm evenings, the amber-green species

May spread out over a thousand yards square,
An island made of bright individuals
Who usually live in the depths, a zone where
Wave movement ceases. Only on nights
Like these do the comb-bearers
Rise, when the bay lies still as a sheet of slate.

Loveliest of sea beings, the color
Of spring arbutus or pink anemone,
As some pass beneath the surface of the water
The effect is of rainbow glory
More seductive than moonlight
To the naturalist who might try to scoop one up

Ever-so-gently in his fine net and
Hold it awhile in a clear beaker of brine—
Perhaps the giant of the race, "Venus's girdle,"
Come from the Mediterranean—
An iridescent ribbon
Which vanishes en route to the laboratory.

The advantage of their luminescence
Is unknown, being of doubtful value in
Luring prey. As for mating: it is difficult
To imagine that these delicate,
Melting creatures could sustain
The violence of love making. Yet they make light.

Dead Reckoning

Halfway between the familiar harbor
And our destination, soon it seemed
Partway between nowhere and nowhere;
The stars we counted on to plot our course
Fled before a mass of ghostly clouds.
And there was nothing more to guide us
But the ship's log and compass,
A scribbled record of our starting out
And the wobbling arrow of direction,
Vague tokens of the past and present,
And the sensation of speed and distance
In the puffed sail, the rope in our wake.
As for the future: the vision of a coast
Unknown and indescribable seemed
The more precious the longer we were lost.
Day dawned upon fog as dense as night.
And some, after many days like this
Turn upon each other in blind rage,
Dive headlong from the foretop,
Or drown in grog, forgetting
Why we ever left home, signed on
For such a voyage, to a land unknown
When nothing had been promised beyond hope.

Hope

In winter the crescent moon vanishes
So quickly in the blue, down the horizon,
Between the starry darkness and morning,

Like the hull of a ship without rigging
That I was meaning to load with wishes,
O not for me, my dear, wishes for you,

And you and you, my friends, all of us,
Such cargo as could only ride upon
The silver shell of that hallowed galleon.

I daydreamed, got bewildered by my muse,
Sun on the lace of frost, and fading Venus.
I looked up, and the reckless moon had gone.

The Frame

In the heat of writing about you
In a blank book, my special one,
I skipped a page, wastefully.
When I thought I was through,
Turning back to where I'd begun,

I noticed this white space,
Speechless, peaceful, pure as only
Silence ever could be
Or will be, ever again:
The hush after hard rain,

Of a rosebud blowing open;
The lull that comes darkly
After someone has misspoken
And nobody knows what to say;
The quiet that fills a room

When death visits the house,
As the spirit hovers in place
And grievers have not yet
Seen it rise above the bed
And turn the color of air.

In the rush to finish my verse
About you, I left a space—
An empty foursquare frame.
And there I saw your face,
More haunting than any poem.

The Neighbor's Garden

I am the luckiest man in the month of May
To look out my high window
On such a plot, and a gardener more lovely
Than the columbine, foxglove, and anemone
She tends with her cunning fingers. So rare!
She stands barefoot among bearded irises
Or kneels to weed as they bow to the glories
Of her bright skin, the roundness of a cheek
Her auburn hair pinned at the nape lays bare.

She rises—most graceful when she stands—
Arms loose at her sides, trowel in hand,
Head cocked, pensive, eager but patient,
Waiting for seeds to take root in the ground
Or buds to blossom.
                         Just so, at twilight,
Despite the untold blessings of my life,
I wait for the spring splendor to be ruined
By wind and rainstorm, hail and hurricane,
Leaving bleak relics, thistle, straw, and chaff.

I hear tomorrow is her wedding day.
A verdant faith glows in her mild eyes.
She clips some roses from a trellised bush,
Suddenly shades her vision with one hand,
And looks up at the window where I hide
In shadow. Laws of light and darkness say
She is the body visible, not I;
And yet she waves to me, the smiling bride.
Hello, my darling, good luck, and goodbye.

Alice

She had come to the place
Just shy of womanhood,
Seeing and being seen
Lovely of form and face,
That cannot come to good
Without some sheltering grace.

Men would stop and stare,
Then turn away, ashamed
Of what they dare not do
And where they might not go,
If madness could be blamed.
Free of pride and vanity

As if she'd been born blind
Or never held a mirror,
She passed in her summer dress,
So oblivious of her beauty
She might search for its likeness
Behind the looking glass and not before.

The Lady Slipper

Into a virgin wood west of Terra Alta
You took me one afternoon in May
To see the bed of lady slipper orchids.
Since girlhood you had kept them secret
So that one spring day you might
Go there as a woman with a man
And find the wild pink orchids blooming still.
You were seventeen; I was a few years older.

In a muslin blouse tied with red ribbons,
You led me by the hand, laughing,
Past cranberry bogs and deep into the pines.
And if I thought you were too young,
I had no heart or mind but to follow you
And see those flowers beloved of Venus,
So delicate and rare they scarce can bear
A man's gaze, let alone the human touch.

In the shade they glowed, the colony
Of flowers, each rising on its green fuse
Out of a crotch of deep-ridged oval leaves,
Each rose-pink blossom with its sac-like lips
Around the pouch netted with purple veins.
And when I turned around, we both were naked.
We made our bed in the hurrying light
On a knoll of moss above the bed of orchids.

Ronsard's Dream

O wouldn't I love to be the golden rain
Drenching the bare thighs of Madeleine
As she sleeps, or tries to, in the downpour;

Wouldn't I love to be the great white bull
Who takes her as she goes over the hill
In April, a flower amazing the other flowers;

Wouldn't I love to slake the thirst of lovers,
Play Narcissus, making the nymph my pool,
And plunge into her all night long;

If only then that night could be eternal,
And dawn kindly refuse to rekindle
A new day—and mine be the last song.

Obsession

I study the hours on an heirloom watch,
Precious hours marked with diamonds
That scatter the sunlight over the room.
Since you left, I am obsessed with time,
Unsure if it is my enemy or my friend,
Knowing that all suffering ends in time.
I wonder if minutes might be redeemed
To some purpose, palliative and kind,
By watching them pass under the second hand;
Or spill in a silver stream through the hourglass,
The wavering thread of sand creating
A pyramid of minutes from its domed tower,
Where a phantom finger gently pushes down
On the white drift until the hour is over.

The hands of the pendulum clock atone
At noon, point to the zenith where the sun
Looks down upon our garden. Alone here
I ransom an hour of daylight,
Hovering over the gnomon of the sundial.
I'm furious at time, which has no end
And no beginning, no heart or balm to heal,
Blind with grief, sun-stricken and unable
To tell by sight an enemy from a friend.

In Late November

Of the butterfly bush, whose purple flowers
The monarch and the swallowtail
Sipped in August, near my windowpane
(Such a wealth of wings and flower clusters
I could hardly see the grass, the trees)
Only stalks and branches remain,
And panicles tipped with russet berries.

Now I see everything so vividly:
The young woman on her hands and knees,
Planting the meek shrubs three years ago—
Three short years and thirteen feet below—
Told me the light was perfect here and so
The plants would thrive, just wait and see
How gracefully the flowers would bear wings.

I would see her when she was not there,
Then go blind, standing right beside her.
How could I begin to explain such things?
Soon enough the blossoms reached my sill,
A floor above her terrace flat. Too late
For her to see the wonder she had wrought
Or for me to tell her. She'd moved out.

I never dreamed these branches in full bloom
Would all but block the summer view below:
Garden, gardener and terrace door,
Casting a dappled shadow across my room.
I never knew that when November came
I would miss the butterflies so much
And see the world more clearly than before.

The Everlastings

In a stream of midmorning winter light
The lavender spray your silver ribbon bound
Hangs upside down from a pin, as bright
As any blue we ever saw in the garden.
With such great gifts, I suppose you might
Have done the same with your strawflower,
Or "cupid's dart," any everlasting,
The fire amaranth with its scarlet leaves,
The globe amaranth, or "love-lies-bleeding,"
With its drooping tassels of red flower spikes
That feel like chenille to the touch.
Such names! Who but a heartbroken
Gardener would make up such a name?

Some ancient Greek named a pure fiction
Amaranth, the myth of an unfading flower,
Never supposing you might make it real
By picking these blooms just as they open
From the bud, before light can turn them brown,
Stripping the leaves, hanging them upside down
In bundles like this one hugged by a band
Until the heat of hearth and home has drawn
The last pearl of moisture from the stems.
For love you left me the lavender, fragrant,
And kept for your own the crown of amaranth
By which, in keeping with an ancient spell,
You've turned immortal and invisible.

Edna St. Vincent Millay

(1892–1950)

Unquiet spirit, by what right
Do I come to disturb your dust
In this omniscient October light
A half century almost from the day
You tumbled down your library stairs
Into eternal night? By what right
Do I invade the dignity of your house,
Ransack the closets, shelves, and drawers,
Measuring your dresses and jewelry,
Picturing you alive, challenging me?

I breathe deep, hoping a sweet scent
Of you, long breathless, might arise,
Some stray atom of your spirit meant
For mine alone. We are not so different
Maybe—man, woman, alive or dead,
Souls confronting the inarticulate.

I come to write your life, a ghoulish trade—
Like others of my time and not like you
Who made a fortune making Fortune rhyme.
To make my living I must turn to prose.
This is what has brought me to your house,
Gardens, letters, grave, and diary.
And if you didn't want biography,
Why do you preserve all of this stuff,
Your books, shoes and teacups, lingerie,
A hat made from a peacock, golden coat
Cut from a lion or an ocelot?
The fiery swirl of hair clipped from your head
In childhood to make tresses for a doll;
The doll itself! Sits staring, cracked and bald
Above the bureau where the hair is kept,

The relic of a goddess, wrapped
In tissue, the red hair that drove men mad,
Made them write love letters by the yard,
Pleading, jealous, tormented by need,
Ready to die or kill for love of you.

You kept them all. Had you no regard
For the dignity of the dead, no modesty?
Did you mean to burn them before you died?
I want to think you left the hoard for me,
Calling me to bring you back to life,
Dangerous, voluptuous, green-eyed:
Better a poet, moonlighting biography
Than a shrunken scholar, deaf to prosody.

I want to believe it. But who am I
To climb this wooded hill
Along an overgrown, untrodden trail,
To touch the gravestone planted in
The earth that owns your ashes still,
Joined with your husband, your true love,
Here in this mountain laurel grove?

I bow my head, a living question mark.
The world was yours: beauty, love, and fame,
The gift of speech, moments of ecstasy,
Money and men, houses, horses, land.
Why, Edna, were you never satisfied?
Can I write what I cannot understand?

I have yet to check the one-room shack
Where you wrote a libretto and a book
Of verse before your beauty and your art
Gave in to gin, morphine, and despair.
Heart pounding, I loose the rusted lock.

Nothing here but a table and chair,
An iron woodstove and a wind-up clock
On the windowsill, faded, vague with dust,
Whose hands were tied one autumn afternoon
Or early morning fifty years ago.
At last! Is this the sign I begged for, some
Sympathetic magic, a poet's trick?
Across the timeless space I hear the rhythm;
The clock, true as a heart, begins to tick.

Now you tell me what you learned too late:
True joy, like genius, is a grace
To nurture, bring to blossom and bear fruit
In its own season. Thundering ecstasy
Always may be bought for the right price
Of wine or the poppy, sex or poetry.
Death to the soul that cannot see
The difference. Lightning blasts the house
Built to be the home for happiness.

The Widower's Journey

In and out of the mountain,
I ride on the railroad train.
As the coach lights go down,
My inward eye recovers.
Day funnels into darkness,
Then tunnels to light again.
Across from me two lovers
Are using the gloom to kiss.

I am untroubled by this.
But something is troubling her,
I think. He is uncertain.
The future is dark to us . . .
A mercy! I long to say
(Too shy for the intrusion)
We see sorrows one by one.
But this is not my play.

He answers whatever she asks,
His smile overturns her frown.
Tragic and comic masks
Overlook the stage curtain:
One fears it will come down,
One laughs that it must open.
The train rolls under the mountain
Where all of us travel alone.

The Glass House

Where should I cast my sorrow
If not here beneath these maple trees
At the lake's edge, with a wishing stone
The cold weight of my heart,
Wishing what has come might be undone?
In the glass house of dawn

Where shall I cast my cracked pebble:
At my own image rising from dry grass,
Purple loosestrife, asters, and goldenrod,
Or beyond, where black water limns a cloud
Rainbow-winged, like a truant angel,
Or drowns the sparrow on the bough?

His song goes rippling on in trills
No lake can trace or echo.
Like the morning mirrored in the gloom,
The fallen world defies the world of grace.
Where shall I cast my stone
If not at the dark portrait of my face?

The Sleeping Messenger

As if a god had crushed the firmament
Into a glittering ball,
Then spread the chart as a portent,
Heaven is in chaos. Let the prophet
Go blind, he will shed no light on it.

The old messenger has his directions
To warn us of gales at sea,
Rape in the hay, the freak accidents
Of birth and death, faithfully
To bear the valid letter of reprieve.

But time has overtaken him in his course.
His eyelids are heavy with the grief
Of so much failure, so many miles.
Hours away, the day dawns on catastrophes
While he sleeps under a crinkled map of stars.

The Good Doctors

July: blue sage and lavender heal the earth.
And I have written not a rag of verse
Since April Fool's Day, when the doctors
Said because of an accident of birth,
A stray gene, some rare glitch in the brain
My boy might never reason like a man.
For me it was as if he had died,
Someone I had loved but never known.

Under the harsh lights, none of us could hide.
Because he could not talk or ring a bell
Like other toddlers, put the peg in a hole,
They had removed his body from its soul,
Probing for the mind that binds us all.
And it seemed to me unspeakably cruel
This child, with a great heart and a smile
Everyone who sees must repay in kind,
Should lack sufficient wit to tell—
In this world of falsehood and delusion—
Good from evil, wise from senseless men.
It seemed unthinkably cruel,
And I lost the cadence of a season
That April day in my grief, a broken fool.

Psalm of Pernette Du Gillet

The night was so dark it had hidden heaven
And earth from me. To my despair,
At noon I could not see a human face,
Though I heard voices. So when dawn
Came rushing in, as if from nowhere,
With its thousand colors, and suddenly
I was surrounded by light, better late
Than never I joined in praising the glory
That led a new day through the broken gate.

The Clockmaker

Time should be heard as well as seen,
Says the clockmaker, carving a cuckoo bird.
My wife gives the sick child his medicine.
Who said children should be seen, not heard?

I work all night until my sight is blurred,
At this abandoned craft that now is mine
For all the comfort folly can afford.
Time should be heard as well as seen.

I can't imagine what life might have been
Without the babies crying, had I preferred
The cloister or the study at nineteen,
Thinks the clockmaker carving a cuckoo bird

In hours stolen from sleep, pleasure deferred
For the sake of this obsession, a daft machine
That never can refund the cost incurred.
My wife gives the sick child his medicine,

Praying he'll sleep soundly and be fine
Tonight or tomorrow night, someday. The third
Time he cried out wrecked my whole design.
Who said children should be seen, not heard?

I dreamed he lay so peaceful that the Lord
Himself believed the stillness was divine
And would not wake him, although my absurd
Clocks froze and went silent for a sign:
          Time should be heard.

The Clock at Wells Cathedral

So time might fairly be heard or seen
By all—the deaf, the blind, the simpleton—
Artisans once made clocks without hands.
Then the clock-jacks, painted manikins,
Came to strike these bells of copper and tin
Within the transept. *God cannot replace*
The quarter-hour lost, and God is good,
Bells remind the blind. Others behold
Two mounted knights ride out and then
Tilt their tiny lances at each other.
Six hundred years in wartime and in peace,
Father and son, grandchild and grandmother
Have brought their kin (also the child within),
To watch one knock the other off his horse
At the stroke of the hour, the winner
And loser always the same, never the worse.

Omega

All day long my watch has been stopping
On me, every few hours, a good Omega
Automatic chronometer, certified,
Gold face and bezel, circa 1970,
Self-winding. My father left it to me
When he died, and never has the watch
Given me a minute's trouble. Maybe
Today I'm too still to keep it wound,
And it's much later than I thought;
Lost hours are shimmering into twilight.
I shake the timepiece, it awakens. I set
The hands that promise to keep moving,
Listen to be sure that we're still ticking.

He Makes His Mark

(for Nathaniel)

Back when only holy men could write,
The farmer or squire who signed himself
With the letter *X,* St. Andrew's cross,
Would bow and put his lips to it,
Reverently, in proof of his good faith.
Now: here's a boy knows only goodness
And honesty. Nature has denied
Him the gift of reason, yet he has made
His mark in the world. Guide
The pen as he scrawls, and bear witness.
His cross shall serve for a name and a kiss.

Lullaby

I sang to each of my children
When sleep came too slowly,
The words of a mystery
In a haunting minor tune:
Open the door softly,
I've something to tell you, dear.
Open it up no wider
Than the crack upon the floor.
Open the door softly,
I've something to tell you, dear.
I learned it from a street singer
Who promised me the rest
As soon as he could remember.
Now I hear he has died.
So I may never hear
Who knocked, who was inside,
What one had to say and why
The other would not open.
And not one of my children
Entranced by the lullaby
Ever turned in my arms
To ask what was unspoken
On the edge of oblivion.

Ponte Verda

In the lightning-crazed sky above the sea
I cannot tell the angels from the clouds
Or any god's voice from thunder.
I have not had the heart for poetry
In half a year, being too much consumed
With birth, death, the hazard and the odds,
To see or hear the breath of my own wonder.

Not by calculus or strategy
Has anyone attained a paradise;
But standing on the stairway where surprise
Alights with its shower of gold, alive
In the hour extempore, wide-eyed, free
As a dolphin or seagull, one may be
Ready for the gods when they arrive.

Has that passage of exaltation scrolled
By me so quickly I did not catch the sense?
To be free, must we understand the world?
This point flows to a line, the line flows
Into a circle of words. Here I live in it
Day to day, the long rambling sentence
Doubling back on itself, ending in prose.

The Messenger

> The movements of faith must constantly be made by virtue of the absurd.
>
> —SØREN KIERKEGAARD

Neither cherubim nor seraphim
Could bear the order. God Himself
Spoke those dire words to Abraham,
To take his only son into Moriah,
Three days from home. All that way
On foot and ass back, he had to brood
Over the strange commands of Elohim.
They pressed on, father and son (the wood
To roast the lambkin stretched a saddlebag),
And two grown men for comfort or defense.
He was much too old, the boy too young
For such a journey, far from Beersheba;
The rocks hid brutal thieves and murderers
Moved by voices mortal and profane.

All this I saw as I hovered near the earth.
God told him to stab the child to death,
Then burn him on the altar, such and such
A mountain, He said, and His word was law.
Spying the crest God promised, he would not
Let his young friends travel the last mile
With him, but said: "Wait here with the ass
While I take the lad to worship yonder."
Loading the firewood upon his son,
He took torch in one hand, knife in the other;
And as they went the child thought it a game
They played. What a joy to be with father,
Alone at last! Though now his father seemed
A little lost and troubled. "I see the fire,"
The boy said. "Here is wood for sacrifice.
This must be the place. Where is the lamb?"

"God will provide," he replied. So He would.
The boy I think still thought this was a game
As father laid him down upon the sticks
And tied him there—except for the odd light
In those faithful eyes, and suddenly the knife.

All this I watched, and here I drew the line.
I am no special angel. Of the nine
Choirs I dwell farthest below the seat
Of the Most High and those Councillors
Who take their glory straight from God,
Or Powers who rule stars and wind and rain.
Little more than a muse am I, more kin
To Helicon's fair nine than the Lord's Thrones.
I whisper truth and guard the innocents.
Knowing the Lord had more then on His mind
Than one graybeard gone mad with piety,
I took it upon myself to countermand
Words spoken in a fit of jealousy
Of human love (He is a jealous God!).
Quick as a thought I flew to the man's side
And told him lay down his weapon, do
No harm to the child. "Put down the knife
Before he dies of fright or you of grief.
We see you would do anything God says
(Or think He said, for how can you be sure?)
And I am only an angel. Please believe
This word in your ear is equal to the Word
You heard or think you heard three days ago.
And look," I sang, "behind you toils a ram
Caught in a thicket, just as you are bound
In the wilderness of Moriah and your mind—
Between the past and present, death and life.
Give God the beast, old man; embrace your son."

The Suit

My grandfather, nineteen years of age,
Falls from the pages of the unabridged
Dictionary where I keep him pressed,
A sepia print of him in his second suit,
A double-breasted serge. The satin tie
Flows from a knot held by a silver pin.
His second suit. The first, he bought
With six years of savings, pennies earned
As cabin boy, deckhand, and seaman.
The night he put it on and went ashore
Some shipmate cracked wise about the cut
Of the cloth or the man who wore it, that
Somehow one was unsuited to the other,
The one being too fine, the other crude.
Whereupon my grandfather swung at him,
And one blow led to another until the men
Whirled into a blur of fisticuffs and blood,
Fought until their clothing was in tatters.

So now he appears in his second suit,
Bought off the rack in Hong Kong or London
Just after the Great War. He's tough
And handsome, bright-eyed, proud,
Daring the whole world to call his bluff,
Cocksure the clothes don't make the man.

Grandfather's Spectacles

He was not a brawler, or vain,
But came up in a time and class
Where a youth of exceptional beauty
Had to prove himself—man to man—
Time and again. Nearsightedness
Made him half-blind; so at fourteen
He went stumbling to the optician
Who ground him his first pair of spectacles.
Amazed by the view, he walked the streets
'Til dark, taken by leaves, pebbles, and stars,
Then the grin of a bully who demanded:
Drop the "frog-eyes" or he'd die laughing!
And in that fight, the first thing broken
Was the miraculous invention
Of wire and glass that let him see
The world and the cost of clear vision—
Ground to dust in the streets of the old city.

A Sense of Style

And in this frame great-grandmother looks lovely
    In her high-collared satin dress,
So many buttons! A button for every sin, as
    They used to say, and the stone
Cameo brooch that has come down to you, my dear.
    Long past her prime she maintained
A sense of style though somehow free of vanity,
    Unlike the pastor, her husband,
Who perhaps from too much Ecclesiastes,
    The *vanitas vanitatum,*
Was so obsessed with this he would not face a mirror
    Or the dark art of photography,
Said he would die first, which his wife took with a grain
    Of salt, or maybe not—we still
Wonder. But at last, she hired Brady and assistant
    To come to the rectory on
Such and such a date when man and wife were to be
    At home, to take their portrait,
For there must be one for posterity, for all
    To read their lineaments.

And as it happened, this was the very day my great-
    Grandfather chose to breathe his last,
A sad day for his widow certainly, and one
    Of confusion, not least because
The photographer arrived with his glass slides and
    Black box before the mortician,
Whereupon she sat the beloved in his chair, propped so,
    And stood beside him holding his hand,
(See, he looks a little drowsy and ill at ease),
    But she is smiling in that way they do
In the old photographs, having to hold the pose
    For what must have seemed an eternity.

Tornado, 1911

(from a diary)

The inquest was reported in the press,
Words of experts, and eyewitnesses
Like me, one may read when I am dead.
She entered the schoolyard before class,
A frail blond girl, no better or worse

Than the rest of us, my mother said.
Kate shut the gate, put down her books,
Seemed about to join us on the swings,
Although she usually played alone.
Next thing we knew a gust of wind

That spun our hair and made a moan,
Lifted Kate Sullivan into the air—
Her arms extended as if to measure
An adventure of impossible breadth,
Her skirt blown out like a balloon.

The wind carried her higher and higher
As one who had been called to Heaven.
Surely the angel that drew her skyward
Would be kind enough to set her down
In this shaky world, or another, gently?

But it was just a funnel of wind alas
That turned her loose as quick and carelessly
As it had selected her from among us,
Dropped her from a height of thirty feet,
And the earth struck her without mercy.

The Vanishing Oriole

Orioles, common as robins when I was young,
Are going the way of the passenger pigeon
Whose mile-wide flocks two counties long
(According to John James Audubon)
Wheeled and coiled like serpents in the sky,
Shutting out the light of the noon sun.
Now nobody alive has ever seen one.

No hue in nature matches the oriole's breast,
That bright cadmium orange, except maybe
Marigolds when the sun is low. And I miss
The bird's staccato mezzo-soprano,
His pitch, so round and rich, his syncopation.
If he has a fault, it lies in the desultory
Treatment of his theme, a predilection

For chattering preludes and fiddlery before
The main melody—a fine construction.
Half-done, he'll take wing, leaving us to wonder
Who will sing the last notes, and when
And where, and who on earth will listen,
As if there were no end to the generations
Of passenger pigeons, orioles, songs and men.

After Whitman's "Lincoln Speech"

The cannons are all silent as the dead
Of that distant war, buried
Long ago, and their widows and children
Also entombed, burned, or lost at sea.
Now it all comes to this hazy distance,
Earth, fire, and water distilled
In autumn air, the gold of chrysanthemums.

In the jewelbox theater where I toiled
Two years or more in wonder and terror,
As soldier and wound-dresser, prisoner of war,
The footlights have gone out
With the damp-eyed ladies in velveteen
And men in waistcoats looped with golden chains,
Vowing to reduce war to pure science;
Gone into Manhattan's twilight and endless sleep.

The stage where the poet mourned his president
Is bare. Where shall we meet such heroes,
So justly grieved by grief so eloquent,
Or strong-limbed courage in a digital age?

Photographer Unknown, Neuvilly, 1918

The light survives, exploding the north wall,
Splintering the vault above the side aisle,
Beaming upon the immobile white columns.
The church, surprised by so much radiance
Shelters the wounded soldiers, dark as pews,
Wound in army blankets, all equal now
In their suffering—blind, lame, or whole.
Who can tell the living from the dead,
Who suffered in brave silence or cried out
For medicine or mother? Not the doctors
Bending over the bodies, or armed captains
Judging who was ready to march again
Into the treacherous forest of Argonne.
Here the light has outlived the last man.

And what it saves is arbitrary, odd:
A spotted dog limping through rubble,
Some silver wickets of the altar rail,
A ladder angling from a chancel window,
So angels might visit if they pleased.
The altar is piled with guns and medicine,
And above it—as if art must have its say
Even now, in the ruins of a French town—
Hangs a life-sized canvas, a baroque scene
Of the Ascension. Christ hovers in the air
Above the stunned apostles, and His mother
In wide-eyed terror, calls to Him, "My son,
Remember me when Thy kingdom comes,
Leave me not long after Thee, my Son!"
For this was the seventh and final sorrow
Of the Virgin on earth, who then was left alone.

Iraq

I thought the war was wrong,
But stammered, tongue-tied
Between a howl and a song.
Not that the war was right
Or the men who made it just;
But to fight the good fight,
Each one in his way must
Guard what he knows best.

I know the human voice,
Gruff on the battleground,
Viaticum, the widow's cry.
Among these is no place
For political poetry,
Which being both is neither.
Too exacting of humankind
To forgive the lawmaker
Or soldier his assigned
Fault in the disaster.
Too pure and tenderhearted
To bear the weapons of peace
After the nightmare has started,
A poet is unfit for this,
Being more and less than human.
I shall try again and again
To countervail chaos,
Not as a poet, but as a man.

Democracy

On the way to City Hall he took a bribe,
Cash, too little to buy a good automobile,
Enough to pay one son's tuition bill.

When he got out of prison, the same tribe
Who'd courted him in power, and some others
Who'd loved him, couldn't look him in the eye.

Shame may turn wolves into lambs, force
Drunks to become saints, turn thorns by
And by into olives, but no treasury of remorse
Can purchase mercy from our cheated wards.

He wept and prayed, hoping his heart might break.
Spring came. And the lawmaker who had made
Young voters cheer and City Council quake,
Thrilled the ballpark, hawking lemonade.

The Flood

Iam satis . . .

—Horace

Palm trees shade the shores of Delaware;
Crocus and forsythia that signaled spring,
Bloom in winter, vexing the calendar.
What more do we need as an omen?
The last wedge of the icecap melting,
Or hurricanes to overturn a mountain?
People are frightened, recalling the Flood
When Noah built the ark, and a lost god
Drove seal herds over the Pyrenees;
Fish darted among the crowns of trees
Where owls and doves, suddenly homeless,
Once dwelled; deer swam until they drowned.

Maybe the Potomac will rise up
In tidal fury under a full moon, and
Batter the White House and the Capitol,
Flush every rat and serpent from his hole
Out to sea, so we might begin again.
Who among you would be shocked by this?
Our children, if any are left then,
Will curse us when they understand this war.
They shall hear how citizens drew their knives
And guns first upon one another,
Then shipped the young abroad to lose their lives.

Philosophers in a Meadow

Gaston Bachelard agrees
With wind-taming Empedocles:
In the soul's true meadow
No flower will grow
But the pale asphodel,
Which we know also
Flourishes in Hell.
And in the soul's meadow
The breath of wind
Failing to find
Melodious trees,
Must be content
To caress the silent
Waves of even grass.

Eurylochus Recalls the Sirens

When we returned from Hell, that sorceress
Who so loved our captain she set him free,
Feasted us with meat and bread and wine,
Praising us for our great-heartedness:
"In going down alive to the House of Hades
You will have died twice instead of once—
Which is enough for any man to bear."
Sunset. And we sailors all lay down
To sleep by the stern cables of our ship.
But shapely Circe kept Odysseus up
Making love to him for the last time, again
And again, an infinity of kisses, and then
Warned him of the dangers that lay ahead.

Of Scylla and Charybdis I shall not speak,
For there are horrors memory consumes
With the men who are consumed by them.
Six comrades of my youth were plucked aloft
By that she-monster with six grinding mouths.
No mercy there, except their death was quick.

The Sirens cut the wound that would not heal.
Circe warned us of these cruel daughters
Of a sea-god, with the heads of lovely women,
And wings and feet of birds. They dwell
On an island near the whirlpool of Charybdis
Where they loll in a flowering meadow, waiting
For ships to pass. They know when to spring,
For Zeus has given them knowledge of everything.

Circe warned us not to sheer too close
To these harpies, or eavesdrop on their singing.
Wives and children will not welcome home
Men who've heard those voices clear and true.
Sirens perch on masts like cypress boughs

Of their island home where dead men's bones
Lie strewn, with flesh still clinging to them.
Circe bid us fill our ears with beeswax
To deafen us—all but Odysseus.
Why did she make exception for the man
She loved, why did she think he might
Listen harmlessly to what would kill us?
"Lash him to the crosspiece on the mast.
And when he begs and prays that you release him,
Tie him all the tighter the more he pleads."

The sorceress conjured up a favoring breeze
That swept us toward Sorrento and our fate.
Suddenly the bowl of the sea grew calm
As if it were a pond on a summer day,
And not a breath of wind to strum the water.
So we stowed the sails and set to rowing
While our captain carved a wheel of wax
Into wedges with his knife. In sunlight
He kneaded the wax and gently sealed our ears.
We tied him to the mast, and went on rowing.
Soon the Sirens mulled the air with music
Soft at first like a maiden's secret humming,
A serenade, or young mother's lullaby:
"Come, come, famous Odysseus, whose name
Brings eternal glory to the Achaeans,
Come listen to our ethereal harmonies.
No man with ears to hear can pass us by,
For wisdom sings the counterpoint to pleasure;
By Zeus, you shall know the past and future."

If the stars could sing in their heavenly courses;
If soft wind could intone the harp of branches;
If nightingales had accompanied Orpheus,

After the Sirens, they would seem like noise.
The maiden's chorale, the lady's serenade,
At last the rainbow of the coloratura
Pierced the melting beeswax of my ear:
So sad a beauty steeped in tragedy,
The melting minor strain of a threnody.
I heard little, yet I heard too much.
Meanwhile Odysseus, the honored guest
Screamed at us, cursed, and chafed and writhed
As if he would tear free of his own skin,
Cried "Mutiny!" commanding we let him go.
I must say this was a vexing test,
As we were duty-bound to serve our captain.
But a voice inside us or above,
Made us true to more than the moment;
And so we tied him faster to the mast,
And bent our oars to escape the Sirens' sound.
So that curious danger, at least, was past.

Many a good man's death I have forgotten,
But not the Sirens' song. It seemed to pass
Into my heart although my ears were sealed.
I have no gift to set the melody
To words, but know the theme right well:
Of love lost, anguish, and the future gone.
Sometimes I hear the exquisite refrain,
Though kindly it grows fainter every day,
As if time and distance from that isle were one.

I welcome the hour that echo will die away.
As for our captain: Circe must have known
Her hero was not like the rest of us—
He could hear that tune with an open ear,
Banish it from his mind and not go mad.

Perhaps it was by grace of the Goddess
Athena, who dearly loved Odysseus,
And served him night and day as guardian.
As for me, I am a simple man
And welcome our voyage into the dark silence.

The White Quill

I sit on a rude bench under the maple tree,
Watching sunrise open up the garden,
Dry the dew from the lawn, then turn
My dark windows above to glaring gold.
High overhead a squirrel is scurrying
Back and forth on a limb, with twigs
And leaves in his mouth, just frantic
To finish making his nest in the tree fork.
A few lyrate leaves rain down on me,
Stems corymbed with winged samara seeds.
My mind is on the character and fate
Of the man who toils behind one window,
Cloaked in darkness, then by dazzling light,
His crimes, lies and folly, work half done.

Here I am and there I am at once,
Spectacle and spectator, audience
And actor in a play without denouement,
Although I know how every knot was tied.
He sat under this tree before he died,
A squirrel above him scolding:
Get to work, you fool, winter is near.
Listen, man, there's no one behind the gold
Windowpane. That room is now for rent.
Look up and see what's drifting down to you,
Gliding and twirling on the autumn air:
A pale feather, longer than your hand,
White from pointed shaft to silken vane.
What kind of bird would drop from heaven
Such a pure quill, too large to be a dove's,
Too small and late for your great apology?

Old Man in Sun and Shadow

Of all my worldly goods and society,
Nothing is left but a table and chair,
A lamp casting dim light on a dark book,
And a grinning skull that will outstare
My blinking gaze unto eternity.

I gave my house to the homeless,
My money and shoes to the poor.
If that brings them no balm or happiness,
They are no worse off than before.
I gave my friends to each other,
My enemies to themselves. I pray
No favor of God or man except
Sunlight and silence where I might find
Some way to slow the minutes of a day,
Save motes of hours from Time's wind.

What have I given that I should have kept?
What have I kept I should have given away?

On a Theme of Ronsard

We die, then the rolling tide of years
Sweeps our works away all in due time.
God alone lasts. Of the human loom,
Not a vein or sinew survives death,
Not a thought or feeling. The remnants
Are loose bones quartered in a lonely tomb.

Soul's joy is to behold God's radiance
And study its source; soul has no essence
But in this restless contemplation.
Happiness has little to do with this;
It comes from making family and verses,
A home, a garden, decent government,
None of which can gain a line or limb
From dust of those whom death has sent
Below. Therefore the bodiless realm
Of the hereafter has no police or laws,
No cities, jails, or theaters—no applause.

As for me: give me thirty years of fame
To revel in the light of the sun,
Good red wine and a woman for loving;
Let the Devil take the century of renown
After the sunken grave swallows my name.
Once a man has passed beyond the days
When he can be moved and not just moving,
What is left has no more need of praise.

Heading Home

I watched the miles, I saw my life go by,
A drumbeat of bare trees and frozen ponds,
Forlorn stations, ruined factories.
I must have dozed, my head against the glass.
Women I dreamed I would have died for once
Mourned me in a dream. South by southwest
Our train cleaved the horizon, pushed the sun
Toward somebody else's sunrise, while
Heaven and earth denied my day was done,
Painting a fantastic continent
Of cumulus and ether, air and mist,
Real as any land to a waking man.
A wall of purple hills sloped to the shore
In fluted cliffs; cloud archipelagos
Edged with golden beaches jeweled a sea
Bluer than our sky. Had I missed my stop?
Now was I on my way out of this world,
Alone on the express to Elysium,
Lotus trees, the lost woman of my dreams?

Shadows deepened and the speeding train
Rolled on into twilight. Slowly then
I came to myself, cold, woke to the thought:
This is how it must be at the end of the line.
You cannot tell the water from the sky,
Mourners from the dead, or clouds from land.
The fire of the sun has tricked you blind,
And earth, air and water join in one.

Codicil

Vain men postpone their wills
Despite all rhyme and reason
In the toll of the church bells,
Thinking to outwit fate—
Because no sensible person
Would trust his gifts to the state.

But this happens every day
As the superstitious scheme
To hold Death at bay
Delays the signature
Meant to rescue and redeem
Control over the future.

My children, I write to you,
Being of sound mind,
As far as a man can know.
I am not rich or poor;
I am neither cruel nor kind
But your thinking makes it so.

I gave you life and give it again
Each dawn, the earth, and stars,
The wind, the sun, and rain,
The choice between good and evil.
I gave you sisters and brothers
To love. Think of me as you will.

From *The Traveler's Calendar* (2002)

Bobolink

You rise from dry meadowgrass
		With a laborious flutter, more
Wing-action than the shortness of your flight
		Would seem to call for

And so it seems obvious
		Flying for you is a steep effort
Nature exacts, though not without amends,
		Bobolink, reedbird;

The wiry tones of your song
		Set forth a waltz in clear whistles
At first, so well-sustained! But then you break
		Down the bars, stampede

Your notes into a reckless
		Song fantasia piped at lightning speed
No one can follow—not the barn swallow
		Who soars with such grace,

Not the bird-watcher stalking
		The field, not blind Tom with all his skill
At sound-catching, his passion for filling
		Darkness with music.

Ricebird, reedbird, bobolink,
		Your song is the strained apology
For all of the weak-winged, condemned to sing
		Because we cannot fly.

Equinox at Newport Farms

Winter deceived us. Now the March wind
Heckles the weatherboarding of the barn,
Drives the weathercock out of his mind.
Poor counterfeit! He can't tell north from south
Or night from day now they are equal and
The lamb's head is in the lion's mouth.

A heron or a heron's ghost in the mist
Wades the marsh, hieratic, Egyptian,
An elegant, high-stepping egoist
With the rare balance to stand alone
In cross winds, still as a bird of iron:
An emblem of long life, so I've heard.

Yet, pinned to the cupola, that painted bird,
Wind-drunk, sun-blind, man-made,
Will outlast him—and me, too, I'm afraid—
An emblem of human thought awhirl upon
Its axis, fanning the compass for direction
While the world ponders, turning in precession
Of the equinoxes, framing an axial space
Like the veering spindle of a spinning top.

Winter deceived us, making us embrace
The long darkness, the hopeless horoscope.
Now something about this vernal equinox
Piques my Libra nature, my need to balance
Future darkness against the daily light.

Neither old nor young at forty-six,
I study the hunting patience of the herons,
The mad persistence of the weathercocks . . .

What days will come to equal the coming night?

The Cataract 9/11

Lately the world seems darker,
Especially in the evenings,
And I light more lamps
To see no better than ever
Familiar faces and things:

Wayworn works of Art,
Books known almost by heart.
Is this the cataract, what
The Romans used to call
A portcullis or waterfall

Descending to subtract
From the sum of my seeing?
A fine word for a hateful thing,
Though now the doctors say
They can lift the veil in a day.

Who takes joy in the word
For a blur that steals his light?
The power is its own reward
And a gift of second sight,
This joy to build a tower,

Without fear or self-pity,
Of words for the horror
That attends the end of light,
A castle to stand bright
In the ruins of a city.

The Lion Tamer at 2:00 A.M.

The crowd is always on the lion's side
    Against the man with the whip.
They wish the spangled girl would slip
    From her spotlight on the trapeze
And fall like a meteor on the ringmaster.
    The inner eye turns glory to disaster.
Hard to survive this art, harder to please.

Always the danger there is not danger enough
    To kill, the spice the crowd prefers to love.
But do not call that preference cruelty,
    Which is just human nature.
Great success leads all too soon to failure
    As men make nature bow unnaturally.
While I put old lions through their paces,

Fathers get bored, the children become restless,
    Hoping against hope I will be mauled,
For they have paid to see the risk, and want blood.
    The art they applaud side-steps violence,
And this is why they go home from the circus sad.
    How can I make a show with ten tame lions?
I'll need five rude savages to save the act.

The Illustrious Critic

For all of us outside his cage, his contempt
    Is nothing less than regal, magnificent.
He will not condescend to a boyish antic
    Like the chimpanzee, to win our applause.
He will not beg like the bear or elephant;
    And he will never display the pacific
Philosophical accession to his fate
    The weights the flesh of a hippopotamus.
He is stark hunger, circling an emptiness,
    The tiger that cannot kill or procreate.
Lord of a realm above rage or gratitude,
    He would as soon eat the evil as the good.

On the Official Biography of Ronald Reagan

On a cold October morning
Venus leads me to work,
Her smile high in the dark,
Bright as a street light.
Up late last night, reading
Edmund Morris, then Horace,
Quintus Horatius Flaccus,
I thought of the poet's burden
To teach and delight,
No matter how little one knows
Or how much joy one is given.

Fear for the generation
So bedazzled few can see
Light between thought and fact
Or that autobiography
And history each must protect
Its realm as best it can.
Patience with a young man
While he revels in folly may
Please God and the Devil
While students find their way.
But the pundit of forty who still
Professes the world is no more
Than his dream or mirror,
And all opinions are equal,
Is worse than a fool and a bore.
Such discourse puts us in peril.

Grant him his place in the sun.
What lately have I done
To winnow right from wrong
Among men who revile the Truth
And lie with every breath?
Did I sell my soul for a song?

The Genie

I do not recall who trapped me in that darkness
The world knows as a vessel of light,
By what cruel trick or Asian sorcery
I was sucked out of this life like smoke
Into that bronze flume, then knocked about
To serve some adolescent fantasy,
Borne down and upstairs, up and down
In a poor boy's hand. Sightless, I was aware
Of jewels glowing on the trees in a dim cavern,
His desire, the mansion, the King's daughter.
And my magic would fetch him all of this,
Though I must be the blind slave to his master,
Free only to serve, benighted otherwise.

I don't know what my lot was like before,
Though it must have been a life of service,
Good deeds and example after a youth well led.
It is far too long ago, a man's age or more.
For when the boy had gained all he wished for,
The vessel that was my crypt got lost at sea.
And the tides shouldered me along the littoral
Many summers and winters, by sun and starlight
In view of cottage, belvedere and beacon,
As I drifted out of time yet ever mindful
Someone on the beach might spy the lamp
Gleaming in spindrift, tangled in sea wrack.
I weltered, mured in dreams, longing and spite,
Blind rage over the world that was denied me—
Houses, wives and children, books and fame—
Redoubling the diabolical vow
If ever I saw the light of day again
I'd use the power solitude had won me
For vengeance against the masters, all vain men,
Even the luckless wretch who set me free.
Curse him, and stop his heart at the next beat.

Plans drawn in darkness fade in the daylight.
As I might cup my own cheek with my palm
To prove if the dream be real, my liberator
Rubbed the carapace of my little prison,
That coffin, the ship that bore me from the past
Onto this dazzling, unfamiliar shore,
The white caress of waves on the sand's thigh
Under clouds like tattered sails of galleons.
In this light I met a man as old as I,
As sad and bitter, who wished only to set me free,
And nothing remains of my passion but the pity.

The Glories

(Antonio de Ulloa, 1716–95)

You that look to nature for the truth,
Consider the indigo mountain, measureless;
Consider the angel flying over the mountain,
Dressed like a star, an eagle or a man.
Antonio de Ulloa at daybreak
Stood with six companions on the peak
Of Pambamarca buried in a cloud.
The rising sun dissolved this to a mist,
A scarcely visible scrim. Due west
No more than thirty yards from where he stood
Each traveler saw, as in a looking glass

The perfect image of himself, his head
At the bull's-eye of three concentric irises,
Rainbows glowing yellow, green, and red,
Encompassed by an arch the hue of silver.
Antonio waved. His spectre followed suit,
Waving, leaping, bowing courteously,
Blind to the wonder of the traveler.
Each man beheld the angel of himself
Shimmering in a glory it could not see
For gazing at the mortal on the mountain,
The shadowed master, backed up by the sun.

This was remarkable to the scientist
Who wrote down the tints of the aurora,
Flesh color radiating vermilion,
Orange turning yellow, fading to straw.
But what seemed more remarkable was this:
Though they stood together, brothers in Christ
Watching these glories appear and fade away,

The sun shone with such natural discretion
    Each of the seven saw his apparition
As if it were a private, holy vision,
    As if one stood alone on Pambamarca.

The Lightning and the Key: A Letter from William Franklin to Joseph Priestley*

(June 7, 1802)

Exile to exile, England to America,
Driven hence by nothing more than faith
In our convictions, we commune once more,
Old friend, man of science, man of God.
Here they torched your house, there they burnt mine.
Here your people fear your love of France—
Marat, Danton, and the bonnet rouge—
As mine once feared my fealty to the Crown.
Hail, fellow, outcast across the sea!
And thanks abundant, deep, long overdue
For such words as you imaged up to spice
That sky-high tribute to my poor career
Splashed in the magazine a few months past.

Now England numbers me among the great,
"One who stood undaunted before the storm."
Half my old royal wage I draw in praise,
Then pension of five hundred pounds a year.
And so I wait for night without complaint,
Grateful for such grace as sunlight yields
On a London balcony in early summer,
And letters such as yours that bid exchange
For welcome sentiments a bit of lore,
The legend of a boy, a kite, a key.
Otherwise the tale would die with me.
Such kindness from you, my father's friend—
(Whose friendship ever joined me to my father)
My late father, whom I mourned early and late,
As reft from me by politics before God—

* William Franklin (1730–1813), son of Benjamin Franklin, was the last royal governor of New Jersey. Joseph Priestley (1733–1804) was a noted English theologian and scientist, and an advocate of the French Revolution.

Such kindness in the twilight sounds as sweet
As posthumous blessing from his troubled ghost.
With all the trackless universe to roam,
I think he haunts the same old firesides
Creaking floorboards with his buckled shoes,
Or stealing the owl's voice to interrogate
Whoever, wakeful, might be listening: "Who!
Who's there? Remember me? Who am I now?
Who was I when I walked upon the earth?
Did anybody know?"
                                        And so he goes
In cocked tricorne, frock-coat and knee breeches,
Wigged or wigless, his broad bald pate,
His lips curled in delight of wine and wit
And ladies' kisses, heavy-lidded eyes,
First to see us through the double lens
The world first saw a man behind, bemused
As much that he had made the spectacles
As that they made folks stop and stare at him.
And so he goes, my father, in death as life,
Rebel, skeptic, rogue, and scientist.
And who should say, O man of God,
That the spirit who prized perfectibility
And never knew an end of inquiry,
Who should say this one is not improved
By death, who sought to profit by all means?

Joseph, you recall when we were young,
My father and I, how I followed him
And how he doted on this "natural son,"
Made in his image, a few inches taller;
Leaner I was, more "imperial" some did say.
I never knew my mother. He was all to me.

He let me choose my horse, my hat, my school,
Thinking such freedom vital to character.
I would have followed my father anywhere,
And did, even into the cannon's mouth.
As Captain to his Colonel, at twenty-three
I led our cavalry against the French
And Indians on the frontier. When peace came
I followed him as clerk in the Assembly,
Postmaster of the City, then all the land.
I was his pupil, factotum, and friend,
Partner in those famed experiments,
One of which now prompts the letter to hand.
(I know I do digress: the ink runs low.
I meant to answer you forthwith,
About the day we chased the summer storm
For Truth's sake. But this is science too.
Was I not my father's chief experiment?)

I followed him to England as his aide
On the legation. He bid me study law.
I read my Blackstone at the Inns of Court:
"The King can do no wrong, the King
Is absolute, all-perfect and immortal . . ."
The "round Temple," that turreted shrine
To civil liberties, became my Church.
And nightly in flickering candlelight beneath
High hammer-beams of Middle Temple Hall
I dined with the best-born men of England,
All of us schooled to rule as gentlemen.
In this I passed my father, the day I passed
Down the aisle of Westminster Abbey,
I, the bastard son of a village printer,
Called to the English bar. A gentleman.

Well-placed letters from this facile pen
Conspired with well-placed friends to fire the comet
Of my preferment. In the court, my star
Blazed up to eclipse my father's embassy.
I'd followed him to England as his aide,
But led him home to America like a Lord,
By our new King named First Royal Governor.

Now maybe his rage is gone, the furious gloom
In which I found myself darkly confined
Years later, when the world turned upside down.
He tried to pull me with him, lectured me,
Threatened, warned me. I was past all that.
In pride I had become my father's sire,
A Governor for him to rebel against,
Chafe, assail, forswear as boys will do
(My own son, Temple, took his turn with me.)
But that generation's wrath surprised us all,
Epic, continental, none could believe it,
Not I, the Royal warden of a State.
Then that gang of cutthroats in the night
Clapped me in irons, led me like a bear
Through streets and village greens of New England.
Two long years I rotted under guard
In a verminous cell so low I could not stand.
Think of my dear wife dying of grief,
Dead four months before I heard of it.
Then my son turned against me, lured away
From filial love and loyalty by—who else?
His grandfather, the glamorous minister
To France! While my father spoiled my son
With French wine, mistresses, and foolish hope
The boy would be our next great diplomat,
I starved in a reeking solitary cell.

While they brokered exchange of prisoners,
I lay with rats in a hole, buried alive,
Sustained by faith my father would save me
The next week, tomorrow, by nightfall.
I could not doubt him, though the world swears
It never could have held me against his will.
Enough of that! When it served the State
To trade a rebel Governor for me,
I got fresh linen, meat and wooden teeth,
My pension, a new wife and afterlife
In exile, as living symbol, as prodigy,
The most loved, the most hated man on earth.

Now, for your scientific history.
The incident under study is a trifle,
A woodcut of a kite, a squall, a key,
A man in the prime of life and his young son
Chasing thunderheads into a pasture
Behind a cold breath of wind. The storm
Mutters low in its throat. The horizon glows.
The kite soars straight up in the storm's face
Like a wish out of one's hand, a frail thing,
A silk handkerchief tacked to a cedar cross
Riding the draft, a wire at the top
To catch the lightning. For a while
We are just man and child, father and son
Dodging raindrops, watching our joy ascend
Higher and higher the unseen tower of wind,
Equal to each other in our delight,
That shared vision of an ideal joined to us
For a moment, by a sleazy string of twine.
That, we had seen before. But this was science.
Tied to the end of twine was a silk ribbon
He wrapped his thumb in, a non-conductor,

So the charge would not shoot through his frame
Should we have luck and net the beast we stalked.
To snare the fire a key hung at the knot.

Still the silk must stay dry while the twine
Steeped in the electric medium of the rain,
Else the operation's bright success
Would spell death to the doctor. Rain fell
And we waited in a cowshed the miracle,
Tethered, watching our kite through the doorway.
It came before we knew, so subtly
I hadn't the eyes to see it, as the clouds
Closed heavier and darker overhead
And drums of thunder rolled across the field.
The loose twine fibers stood up on their ends
Like fur on a cat's back arched in lethal fury.
"Look, Billie! How the charge excites the line:
Fire enough in the key to fry a mouse!"
But who else would believe it? The iron key
Was dull as when I snatched it from the door.

Here is the part of the story few have heard:
I was not a child then, I was twenty.
I was the man pursued a whirlwind once
As branches and tree trunks flew through the air,
Spurring my spooked horse into a thick wood
Where I caught his tornado—it was my report
That proved his theory of the whirlwind's cause.
I had not his genius, but I was brave, and
Thereby his praise, if not his love, I earned.
"Here father, let them wonder about this!"
I cried over his shoulder, and held the key,
Cutting a brand in my hand no one could deny.
He drew the lightning, I was the one burned.

Magic for Houdini

After the feast in his honor, the magician
Checked his watch, blinked, palmed a yawn,
As amateurs turned water into wine or wine
Into water, and beamed at his applause. Next?
One held a cigarette paper rolled betwixt
Thumb and forefinger, and beguiled
The crowd with faultless patter promising
To turn this sheer paper into a live moth.

Gracefully he rolled the paper. Smiling,
He made a fist. But then the Truth
Upstaged the actor, as it sometimes does.
When he opened up his hand again,
The smile that had been poised above success,
Died on his lips. Where life should have been,
A flutter of fresh wings as the moth flew free,
Death left its ashes, the poor bug's remains.

Knowing the greatest illusion ends in folly
As even the best magicians fail sometimes
To make the incredible act a certainty,
Houdini raised his hands to start a round
Of clapping to mask the man's embarrassment,
A simple trick of professional courtesy
For the thing boldly attempted, bravely lost—
And maybe a little sympathy for the moth.

But then the audience drew in its breath.
A living moth came flying from nowhere
And circled the mortified magician's hair,
Once, twice, three times. Crackling applause
That might have come from pity came from fear.
And no one's dread ran deeper than the master's
Who was all too familiar with these powers
Of darkness. He would be dead within a year.

Collection

I rode a hundred miles in a limousine,
Gun in my belt to capture what was mine.
He knew what was coming. Held the door for me,
Poured the drink I knocked back spitefully.

I told him if he did not pay
Me what he owed I would take away
His car, his house and furniture, his land,
The ring from his finger, finger from his hand.

I told him if he did not pay
Me X amount of cash by Saturday
There would be no Sunday. I would take
One by one the weeks of his month away,

The days of his year the years of his life;
I'd take away his children and his wife,
All he ever dreamed or had not dared
Yet dream, that too, nothing would be spared.

He nodded. When I had gone out the door,
Leaving it open for the night to enter,
I wept because I didn't know for sure
What the man owed me, what I had come for

Or how I'd lived without it for so long.
My rage was old already, the night was young.
Under the cracked laughter of the moon,
I ordered my patient driver to move on.

The Traveler's Calendar

Dawn opens the accordion of facades,
Formstone and striped awnings of a street
Robber Barons paved to lure the drones
Hived in textile mills along the Falls
A hundred years ago.
                                        In my corner room
With a view of row-house cornices and
The ruined forest on the hill beyond,
I keep no clock or mirror.
I want no ticking image to remind
My muse of Time's progress on this front,
The dial of minutes or my quotidian face.
Nothing temporal excites this place
But daylight, nightfall, and the creeping dust,
Metamorphic wind against the glass—
And this eternal Traveler's calendar,
Months adorned by Currier & Ives.

Faithful as Christmas, the agent of doom
Sends me this quaint scroll from Connecticut.
You know the type: a paper monument
To Mark Twain's America, the cake-tin
Rococo sweetness of the Gilded Age.
January snow, the horse-drawn sleigh
Leaving the fields trackless, immaculate;
Skaters testing ice on the mill pond;
Children chasing butterflies in May.
If there is a naval battle in July,
You may be sure it happened long ago
When patriots died gladly for their land.
And heavenly smoke-billows from the cannons
Mingle with clouds to hide the fire and gore.
Always a merry steeplechase in spring,
Always the summer sailing on the Bay,
Cloudless, stormless, happy mirror of blue!

Farmhouses in the lusty light of morning,
Twilight stealing the green hills away;
The October perfection of still life—
Grapes and apples light cannot resist
Touching with silver fingers. Always
The glorious landscape larger than the man,
The boy forever fishing the mountain stream,
Innocent, proud, beloved.
                    America!
Who could forgive or forget your promises,
America as it only could exist
In dreams of men who toiled to barter dreams
For a row-house mortgage, insurance premiums?
Humanity was lost in your vast mood—
A mood-mountain, longed-for, uncertain—
A troubled child that could not come to good,
His passions buried deep under the mountain.
America, who can forgive or forget you?
I revisit the past, I can and I cannot.
Our landscape is stricken, the waterways
Poisoned with chemicals I cannot name,
Our sunsets freaked and stained with iodine.
Nothing looks the same but the pure flame
Of sun at noon. I mourn what was never mine.

The Hartford agent wants to sell me "Life"
For what it's worth to him and my family.
His calendar's a subtle tug at my sleeve,
Or not so subtle, now that I study it.
As if the color plates were not enough
To signify the imminence of Heaven,
Here come the phases of the moon:
January frames the infant's face,
The crescent moon of March a boy of ten

Who, in flowering June, is a young man,
Grey in August, white-haired in November,
Dimples worn to trenches in his cheeks.
Death has made my calendar a mirror,
Flashing the twelve disciples of long life!
Then to remind me of the odds against it,
Death, the engraver, shows me the full moon
Like life in its luminous moment of glory,
Star-crowned, or cloud-adorned, while nearby
Lurks the black mouth of the new moon, saying:

"O live for the glory of the round of light
Crowned by stars in July, or cloud-haunted
In April; but bear in mind the black circle
Of the new moon sailing stealthily among
Your gaudy planets and constellations.
I am the dark round period that waits
Each day for the end of your sentence."

Caesarean

(for TJE, born on Memorial Day)

Startled from ancient sleep in a dark house
By crashing walls, harsh torches, strangers
Dragging him naked through his mother's blood,
No hero would stand up to the invaders
With such intrinsic dignity as you showed
This morning, the first day of your life.
At the shock of air you cried out loud
In sight of a new world, and a world lost.
Then you were quiet, curious, engrossed,
Blue eyes half-open bearing a ripple of light
From that primordial ocean cast asunder.
May your vision never weary of the sight
Of this strange country and our stranger ways;
And may the days be worthy of your wonder.

The Code

I took my son from his weary mother.
I gathered him up and paced the living room
In a grey sunrise crossed by early lightning.
After a little while he stopped his crying,
Lifting his head from my shoulder to look around,
Widening and narrowing his eyes as if
The world were stranger than it is to us
Who have puzzled over all its strangenesses.
My face, to him, is a luminous mystery.
He's not old enough to know just what he's seeing
(I wonder if anyone ever is) but already
He seems to know the code of sound and rhyme.
I heard the faraway murmur of spring thunder,
And my son smiled at me for the first time.

Benjamin, Son of the Right Hand

How many years had I been musing
On that mind-bending Zen koan,
"The Sound of One Hand Clapping,"
When you, from a grown man's height,
Though not yet a man,
Heard us old folks puzzling over it?

You smiled with that calm delight
Only the wise can feel and understand.
Standing tall, you lifted your right hand,
Palm up, the way they do in Italy
When calling "Ciao!" to children.

Tapping your fingertips upon the palm,
You clapped one hand so softly
We bowed our heads to listen.

The Solar Eclipse in the Luxembourg Gardens

(for my son Theodore)

1

Clear vision, and a life so long you may someday
    Arrive in Paris to watch the total eclipse—
May such blessings attend you. Better yet
    You'll be in love, you and your beloved may
Stand in this dappled garden under clear skies
    And watch the miracle in our place.
By then I'll be in eclipse myself, so I send you
    These scattered thoughts as my penumbra.

First, a warning: Don't look at the sun
    Except through Mylar the finest shades
Science fashions in 2081. Our grandfathers
    Who watched the eclipse through their fingers
Learned too late their folly as they lay
    All night in agony, with the "lamp of day"
Blazing in their skulls. Power blinds us.
    So does love. But that is another story,

And now I want to tell you what you'll see
    When you are here, and your mother and I are gone.
Paris will be looking much the same as ever,
    Its bridges and churches reflected in the river,
The lindens fragrant, the dahlias and larkspur,
    Chestnut trees caverning the long black pool
Of the Medici fountain. Lovers gaze into the mirror
    Of still water, at tree branches steeped in azure,

And toward the far verge, the grotto-sculpture where
    Hideous one-eyed Polyphemus hulks

Above nymph Galatea, and Acis, her paramour.
    The cyclops, crazed with jealousy, heaves a rock
Overhead to crush the boy's brains in a moment—
    Which moment has not come in my lifetime
Of bombs, earthquakes, vandals, and civil wars
    And, God willing, will not come in yours.

The group, a *memento mori* or axiom, inspires
    Lovers to treasure glad hours, for always
There is a monster aching to divide us. I meant
    To tell you how to meet the eclipse,
But love broke in, as it will do in Paris, stealing
    The conversation. When you have purchased
Your silver spectacles, you want a vantage point.
    There is no more perfect place than this.

So if clouds come to threaten the sight of Heaven,
    There will be so much to see here in this garden
No one will mind. At midday look for the violet disk
    Of moon behind the blue curtain of sky
To crop out and nick the sun, then for the sun
    To pull the moon on slowly, like a mask . . .
O where will I find the words for what you shall see?
    The birds are mute in this breeze as the air chills

Faster than the fading warmth of a body whose soul
    Has flown. The crowd cries O! Behold the black sun!
See the crown, its arches of flame rising and falling,
    And our winter constellations shining at noon,
Wakened from dreams. As you are about to admire
    The rare dew on the leaves, daylight will return
So quickly you may wonder if you had been dreaming
    And woke to find yourself in your father's poem.

2

Thumbing through Nostradamus, couturier
Paco Rabanne divined the space station Mir
Packed with plutonium, would crash on Paris
This afternoon, torching the whole metropolis.
In a week without much news, it was big news,
So was any millennial hocus pocus
About eclipses—ancient, modern, or to come.

During the cinquecento, Christendom,
Torn by religious wars, took comfort in
Thoughts the solar eclipse would begin
A trend of reversals—the fall of Rome,
Decline of Emperors, Popes Paul and Pius—
Signaled by flood and firestorm, global chaos.
One country priest consoled his frightened parish
By preaching that because of the great rush
For penance, Our Lord in His mercy might
Well put off the eclipse for a fortnight.
We are not so fearful, though the chill wind
Of eclipse draws thoughts of death down
Through centuries of the benighted mind.
Facing the eclipse, all eyes on the sky
May atone for millennia of opacity,
Blind ignorance, which feared the earth,
Moon, stars, and planets. Now our terror
Is turned upon ourselves and one another
And this cosmic pas de deux draws us together
From the Atlantic to the Bay of Bengal.
An old man with the face of an apostle,
Bent forward, looks up through his "lunettes";
In shop doorways, on steps of cabarets,
Everyone awaits the miracle.

At the apex of the march to La Madeleine
A wedding procession halts. Everyone
Looks skyward. Have the vows been said?
Or is the party awaiting the shy bride?
Now you can see no more of the cored sun
Than a hoop of gold. A bridesmaid says
It looks to her just like a wedding ring.
The maid of honor in her pale blue dress,
The army captain whose uprightness
We prize so much in funeral corteges—
All peer at the sun. So does the file
Of mourners bearing a casket to burial
At Père Lachaise, the priests, the widow,
Dark-suited relatives cast in Death's shadow . . .

Then, like a fat man under a bedsheet
Who hides his head, uncovering his feet,
The sun shows on the side where we weren't looking,
And light returns, outspread, the world is glowing . . .
What a concurrence, what a happy chance
The moon is the perfect size, the right distance
From earth to hide the sun the way it does!
It will not be, nor was it always thus
In the full range of eternity. Glorious
That we stand in this garden, man and woman,
Heirs to Paris, the stars, the human eye.

Baudelaire's Swan

(for Richard Howard)

Hard by the Louvre, I think of Andromache
And the poor river that mirrored the widow's pain,
Simois, the faithless river drunk with her tears.
As I watch the Ferris wheel the plot whirls in my brain.

Old Paris is no more. The city changes so quickly
No human heart can keep pace. Now I can see
Only in my mind's eye the hucksters' stalls
Pitched in the ruins of columns and capitals

And gaudy bric-a-brac in the showcases.
Here once was a little zoo. And one morning
Under a cold clear sky in the hour of waking
For work, when traffic's hurricane wrecks the silence,

Baudelaire saw a swan stray from its cage.
Webbed feet slapped the dry concrete
As he trailed along his white plumage.
Near a dry gutter he cracked his pathetic beak,

And bathing his wings in the dust, remembering
The beauty of lost lakes he began pleading:
"Rain, when will you weep? Come, storm and wind!"
I cannot shake that image from my mind.

Paris changes, but my sadness is the same.
New buildings, suburbs, scaffolding, concrete blocks—
Now it's all allegory to me, frame by frame,
And my precious memories weigh me down like rocks.

In this strange city my soul has chosen for exile,
Hearing Memory wind its horn, worn melody,
I think of sailors left on a desert isle,
Forgotten. Vanquished. Captives of Memory.

Gifts

I gave her a golden locket
  To shut my portrait in.
She filled it with a butterfly
  Wing, the blue of Heaven

And wore it until the day
  She turned to me from the mirror
To kiss, and the locket behind her
  Opened and flew away.

I gave her an antique ring
  Some lover had lost in pawn.
She gazed from the sea to her hand
  One night—the diamond was gone.

I gave her a chain of flowers
  That die before they are old.
She will outstay diamonds and gold.
  I will give her nothing but flowers.

From *The Boy in the Well* (1995)

for Benjamin Robert Epstein

At Poe's Grave, Westminster Church

Lovers tread lightly the April grass,
Whisper among tombs, in honor and fear

Of the very souls that might bless
Their passage. This green island

Necropolis in the urban sea
Invites lovers to stroll,

Embrace out of sight of all
But the gentle dead who cannot

Hide their delight, but spin it out
In myrtle, sudden violets, wild thyme.

The stonc lyre wound in laurel
On the cornice of the poet's tomb

Cannot keep still in this breeze
But hums an ethereal chord as

The young woman leans to touch
A stone carved with her initials.

Her lover picks a violet for her,
She raises her lips to his and as

They kiss the breathless landscape runs
Lengthwise through them, vanishing

Into a niche where there is no death,
Past or future graveyard, no dominion

But the bound and indivisible soul.
When at last they come to themselves

Years later—or maybe only a few seconds—
The world returns to April somewhat shaken.

The Inheritance

The night his heart stopped, and my father
Drove the Cadillac haywire into a shadow,
Nobody knew where he'd been. A heap of money
Lay strewn across the front seat as if Death
Had thrown it back in his face;
In the ignition dangled his cryptic keys.

My job: to find the locks for those keys
And what they guarded, a puzzle my father
Left scattered in his wake for me to face.
I had to open the doors under his shadow
Though one might easily open upon my death,
A scene of vengeance, or a vault full of money.

All we ever argued about was money,
His love of it, my disdain. Now the keys
To his kingdom fell to me, as if Death
Had longed to cast me in a role my father
Created, while he watched from a shadow
As I fumbled at entrances he refused to face

At the end. Weary, confused, he would not face
Any problem he could not kill with money:
Adoring women, the law's relentless shadow
That trailed him rattling chains and prison keys,
His failing heart, his curious son. My father
Knew he was dying and tried to buy off Death

With coin of the wrong realm. When Death
Laughed and threw the cash back in his face
It must have been that moment my stunned father
Saw the border of the dominion of money—
And love beyond. Too late to explain the keys
To me as I cried angrily after his shadow,

Too late for me to hear him, once his shadow
Faded into that crowd in the halls of death.
Without a word of advice I got these keys
To a dangerous treasure. I see his lonely face
Smiling upon my grief that all the money
I find won't buy a farewell from my father.

Father, open the door behind the shadow
Money cast between us, and then Death;
Face me, bless the bearer of these keys.

Lost Owl

When the sky is right, the moon and stars
Shine through the window on my son's bed,
Lighting his way to sleep. But last night
He called to me: An owl, he said,
Was singing from the oak tree in our yard.

An owl, I wondered, in this city where
All species are more or less endangered?
"Go to sleep. You must have heard a cat."
"But look!" he cried. "There is the bird!"
So I got up to sit with him in the dark.

On a high branch backlit by the moon
The pointed ears, the round head of the owl
Cut from the sky a perfect silhouette
Which chilled me even though it thrilled my son.
I sat with him in the darkness a long time,

Charmed by his pure joy in the owl's song,
Known for centuries as an omen of doom.
What was it doing outside my child's room?
Singing, clearly, for a captive audience,
I in my fear, my son in glad innocence.

I yawned. The boy nodded. I tucked him in
And went to my corner of darkness, comforted
The patient owl that sang my son to sleep
Was not the owl I dread, not mine, but his,
The kind prophet of a strange new wilderness.

The Book of Matches

Because I could not stay with you forever,
The book of matches each red tip a year
Of marriage flared in the untidy cellar

Next to a bag of gift-wrapping ribbon
And paper which made a restless dragon
Breathing fire, licking the floor joists,

Burning craters, fountains of jagged fire
Up through the living room where the piano
Moaned in a crescendo of broken strings.

Flames climbed a ladder-backed chair, lit
Greedily on books, speed-reading the legend
Of our years together, disdaining the hearth,

Attacking the constancy of a staircase
We climbed one after the other hand in hand
Long after the children had gone to sleep.

Because I could not hold you long enough
The fire wrapped our bed in a cruel curtain
Where our bodies once shone making love

And at last it burst into the children's room
Furious to find them gone, no longer children
Any more than we are bride and groom.

Epiphany

Out in the cold, the contents of a house:
Carpets, lamps and bedsteads, kitchen range,
Holiday litter, bells and tinsel. Strange,
As if a huge hand lifting the residence

Shook it above the street while fingers probed
Corners and closets looking for evidence,
Clues among new clothes, toys, books unread,
And games the children scarcely learned to play.

Who lived here last year, only yesterday?
Cardboard Santa and the Three Wise Men
Pause over the lintel to watch a star
Wink through a flawed cloud. Lost again.

Somewhere tonight a child is being told
There will be a better home for him
In the new year, a warm bed and fresh linen,
Constant love, and new toys for the old.

The Boy in the Well

How brightly the stars shine beyond the day,
Men at work in town, children at school.
Birds twitter in a feathery mimosa,
And ghosts visiting the abandoned farmhouse
Far from town, slip through the fingers of light.

Ding dong dell, Johnnie's in the well,
Deep in the farmhouse well, out of sight
Of all but God's curious, unsleeping eye.
He's fallen far from the wafer of light,
Which hovers above him at the mouth of day,

Fallen down, down the green stone cylinder
To a moist hole where there are no answers
To his cries but his own echo or
A cicada maybe, the prophecy of a crow.
A rope tied to the windlass slipped.

Who put him in? It was his own notion
After the blind beggar in town explained
How from a pit delved deep enough
You could see the stars shining at noon.
So many nights lying on his bed, gazing

At Orion swaggering across the heavens,
The boy would dream he was in a cave,
Warm and wise, watching stars dance
Above the literal day uncommonly bright,
Constellations acting out the old legends.

Down in the well the boy thinks he hears a cicada
Or maybe it's the strange echo of his voice.
How brightly the stars shine beyond the day
Which by now has journeyed far beyond morning.
He wishes on one star with all his might,

That Orion might reach down and save him
Or wake him from this nightmare in his own bed.
He doesn't know anymore if it's day or night.
By now the children have come home from school,
All but the bravest. His mother will miss him.

The Twins

The secret of twins is that they have no secrets
But a code like the jargon of bees
Or the rushing of a creek through grasses
So what is known to one is known to the other.
Falling into step along the beach or boulevard,
Surrounded by light or shadowing each other
The twins project a harmony so perfect
That, to all of us born lonely, destined to struggle
As lovers, parents, brothers, reluctant strangers,
They are a mystery and mild reproof.
We dress them alike, angry over our strangeness,
Envying those blessed to be born separate and one.
On the green seesaw of their delicate incarnation
The twins balance, a perfect closed parenthesis.

The Survivors

After dinner conversation dies
In silence like a spell
No one can break but the enchanted guest.
You are enchanted. Some say you are blessed.
Had you gone with your sisters a year ago
To the river bridge under the moon in April
You would not have returned to tell the tale
Our silence begs for, wishing it were not so.

Sorrow has hewn the innocence of your face
Into planes of enduring loveliness.
You have come east from St. Louis
Fleeing a nightmare retailed by the press.
You've told it a hundred times before
To others, and yourself. Now once more
You gaze into curious faces as a mirror
Judging beauty unqualified by rage

Or terror. Your younger sisters had gone
To write their verses on an abandoned bridge,
To watch the moon's face on the river glow
Rushing in whirlpools ninety feet below.
Your sisters found they were not alone,
Too late. Four men with hunting knives
Pinned the girls to the stone,
Raped, and threw them over, one by one.

Now a second silence closes in
As we measure the imponderable burden.
One pours the wine, another takes your hands.
Our souls devise a span across the river.
The silence answering you is the sea's silence
Rocking grief to sleep, drowning the pain;
Sad verse upon the bridge you must walk forever
From life to death, from death to life again.

The Ferryman

(after a tale of Dunsany)

For him it was not a matter of years
Or even centuries, but wide floods of time
And the ancient heaviness and ache
In his corded arms that had become
Part of the grand scheme the gods had made.
Now if they should send a cruel head wind
How could it help or hinder or change things,
Except to divide all time in his memory
Into two equal portions? So evenly grey
Everything looked where he rowed, if any
Radiance flickered a moment among the dead,
On the face of a Cleopatra or Bernhardt,
The ferryman never would have noticed it.

Yet he did notice and thought it strange
When the dead began arriving in such numbers:
They come in hundreds, sometimes thousands now
Who used to come in dozens, long ago.
His job was not to count, it was to row.
But then for a long time there was no traffic,
And this is uncommon, he thought, for the gods
To send no one down from earth for a decade—
Though gods in their wisdom know what's best.

Then one man walked the pier. His little shade
Sat shivering on the skiff as it pushed off.
Only one passenger: the gods know best.
The weary ferryman rowed on and on
And the river sighed the way Grief in the dawn
Of ages moaned and sighed among her sisters,
A song that could not die like the echoes
Of human sorrow failing on the earth,
Though it was old as Time and Charon's pain.

From the slow river the boat loomed to the coast
Of Hades. The lone passenger stepped ashore
As Charon turned his boat toward the world.
"But wait, I am the last," said the new ghost
Alarmed by Charon's face against the sky—
For no one had ever made him smile before,
No one had ever seen the ferryman cry.

The Cages

On the sixth day of Passover,
The first warm day of the year
The zoo is full of Jews,
Orthodox Jews in gabardine,

Bearded grandfathers, students
Wearing yarmulkes or black
Fedoras tipped jauntily back,
Making the most of the breeze.

Young men push baby carriages
Along the aisle of cages;
Mothers in full skirts,
Babushkaed old women

Lead grandchildren to peer
Into the lion's den,
Eye a hyena and laugh
At the tumbling monkey and bear,

Marvel at the tiger
Whose coat is a tracing of bars,
Those furious pacing jaguars
Measuring their freedom

Under a boundless sky.
Jews of all ages come
Out of the house of bondage
On the finest day of the year

And April sunlight casts
Shadows of iron bars
On the children's curious faces
As they pass among the cages.

Russian Village Suite

(after Marc Chagall)

I. Listening to the Cock

When the world was still
Upside down in slumber
And trees seemed to hang
From the night clouds,
And the claw of the moon
Scratched between silences,
I heard the crow of the cock.
I heard the cock sing
And it was not for day,
Or for night he was crowing—
It was for life.
I heard him cry for
Dear life, which was coiled
Inside him like a hen
Full of eggs while
High above in the night
The barnyard animals
All dreamed of living
The lonely lives of men.

II. The Revolution

O Nikolay, what a show
You have made for the crowd!
You are a living flagpole
For the banner of Revolution!
All eyes are upon you
As you play the acrobat,
Standing on one hand
While the flag waves from your legs!
All the world is watching,

Armies, children, and lovers
As you stand on one hand
On the table where a rabbi
Sits holding the scroll of the Law.
All eyes are upon you, all
But the rabbi's weary eye.

III. The Three Candles

Harlequin tunes his flute
To play for the wedding
A song of blood and fire,
A song to make the dead
Happily dance with the living.
Angels with violins glide
Over the chapel dome
Serenading groom and bride
As they walk above the earth.
A shady angel unrolls
The red carpet for lovers,
The living and dead, to dance
As they pass from innocence
On this path of blood and fire.

IV. White Crucifixion

Lions above the arc
Rise up roaring in pain
As a tongue of yellow flame
Blows from the temple door.
Why is the temple on fire?
Why are the books on fire?
Why must a bearded scholar
Shouldering the sack of Time
Warm his hands at this fire

Of the white scroll of the Law?
Why is our village burning?
In the stream of Heaven's light
The flying dead hide their eyes,
Whispering at the vision:
One of their own on the cross,
His lean and tormented loins
Wrapped in a ragged tallis.

V. The Fiddler

When in the night the fiddler
Flies over the town
Scattering notes like silver,
Tuning birds to a chorus;
When in the night the fiddler
Crosses the strings with his bow,
The church spires stand on tip-toe
To listen, the whistling trees
Shake off the dust of snow;
The stars rub their eyes,
And shake off the night clouds.
And I wish I had three heads,
Three sets of ears to hear
The golden and green melodies
Of the fiddler as he goes by
Leaving footprints on the sky.

VI. In the Night

If God ever speaks to me
It will be on a night like this,
A snowy night in January.
We will be embracing
In the middle of the street,

So dearly in each other's arms
A lonely man in his doorway
May warm himself at our fire. Yes
It will be such a night as this
That I'll hear God's voice,
A night when there is such light
From the knife of the moon
The snowflakes all around us
Tremble: stars taken by surprise.

Beauty and the Beast

He was drunk and twice my age,
The greybeard at the party,
Old enough to declare failure
As husband, father, and teacher.
And as far as I could tell
He was a failed poet as well,
Though his poems were everywhere.
He thought I admired him so
I would be charmed to be taken
Into confidence as he extolled
A beauty smoothing her hair,
Much nearer my age than his:
"She's the one, the one I know
Will turn it around for me,
The woman to save my soul."
I nodded in sympathy knowing
The obvious rule—the man
Who thinks a strange woman can
Save him, is his own doom.
I watched him lurch through the room,
Kiss her hand. A perfect fool.

Ten years later they're married
And he's given up whiskey for tenure
In the Midwest. His wife I hear
Is more beautiful than ever
And kind, clever, and strong. He
Has made peace with his children.
And now that I'm older I open
His book from time to time to see
If I may have been wrong
About some of his poetry.

The Great Pyramid

Miles across the sand the Great Pyramid
Looks like you can touch it. One more step
And the dimensions dawn in grand severity:
A solid sky-long sunbeam rayed
From a split cloud. To shine all day
While enclosing the deepest man-made night
Makes a paradox of fearful weight.
In vastness and terror, we feel the sublime.

Stand on the broken peak. Old images
Rush by: Alexander on his war horse
Who, in passing, gazed at the ancient height
Where once stood Pythagoras, every bit
As moved by these mysteries as the rest of us,
Though he knew life was resolved in harmony.
What he'd heard of the pyramid was poetry
No less baffling for its epic beauty:

Centuries before the flood, a king
Dreamed the earth turned over, burying
Everyone. Stars rang and clashed and fell
In shapes of birds who plucked up men and flew
Between high cliffs that opened wide and slammed.
Waking in the cold sweat of the damned
The king roused his priest whose stars foretold
The deluge, and ordained the pyramid.

Whether the poet-priest meant what he said
Or more, his words became a juggernaut,
A king's hobby and his people's destiny.
Pythagoras, barefoot on the pyramid,
Standing where the point was once pure gold
Till lightning struck, or some colossal greed,
Rubbed his eyes and thought, and stared and thought . . .
A hundred thousand men worked twenty years.

What for? The pile would make a clumsy ark
For all but the most figurative deluge,
Blind waves of oblivion. This stone sunbeam
Might pierce the high tide with its tip of gold
And show a soul to Heaven through the dark.
If death is the negative of what is known,
A world seen in the unknown looking glass,
A pyramid might create resplendent space

By turning the daylight inside out,
Making a tower against nothingness
As indestructible as poetry,
Which men may lose but God cannot erase.
So, in the heart they built a royal vault
And filled the room with charms and jewelry,
Rust-proof swords, rich earth, and poison,
Clear glass that might be bent but never broken;

Stone sentries smiling with hypnotic eyes
Could lure a raider to his last embrace,
Should one trespass. But time in time brought men
Whose souls of alloy idols could not break.
Al Mamun the wise, the seventh caliph,
First to try and westernize Islam,
Used fire, vinegar, and a battering ram
To crack the wall in the first millennium.

Drunk upon the logic of the West
Or youth, which takes each omen for the best,
Al Mamun laughed and led the torches past
Three thousand years of darkness and dead air
To a king lay spooled inside a coded chest
Dreaming the tragic future. A diamond
Blazed on his brow like sun on Pythagoras,
The point of the pyramid his golden mind.

The Hanging Gardens

Words failed him. Knowing her desire,
Beyond love, for the country of her youth,
He toiled in his heart to tell a truth
That defies words. The King told his mason
Raise bridges from nowhere to nowhere,
Arch after arch with terrace cantilevered,
Making his wife an Eden above the plain.

Now from the palace window she could see
An arbored garden on a floating hill
Where she could stroll at will
In shade of a singing pine and lemon tree.
Yet she gazed beyond leaves at the changing moon,
Troubling the King's sleep
Because his labor of love was hardly done.

So the monarch bid his mason raise
Arches on the blossoming tableland—
Then crisscross colonnades on the cornices
So shadows should not drown the garden floor.
Arch upon terrace rose to the seventh level
Where the Queen climbed through the jasmine air
Stargazing, yet far from Heaven as before.

This was the King put prophets in the fire
And boasted he alone built Babylon—
Then found himself upon his hands and knees
Grazing with oxen, banished beyond recall.
Yet Daniel, the Kings' captive oracle
Read this dreaming tyrant well enough,
The golden head, the feet of iron and clay

And led him dream by dream to higher love.
Too late for his Queen. She heard the key
Ring on the threshold of life's last archway

And could not tell a soul the miracle.
Thinking the door to happiness must lie
Outside her time and space,
She climbed the seventh stairway toward the sky.

Phidias in Exile

1

Phidias crowned the Parthenon with stone
Centaurs so real they cracked to breathe.
Sculptor in marble, gold, and ivory,
He hammered up the Athena Parthenos,
Statue of his city's patroness.
But rivals cried that he had stolen gold
Belonging to Athena's draperies,

And only a King could save him. Pericles,
Fearing the Persians more than decadence,
Had ordered the statuary gold all made
In moving plates that once unscrewed and weighed
Proved the hated sculptor's innocence.
Still his furious rivals were not done
Plotting to trip him into hell or prison:

Some critic spied among the warriors
Raging around Athena's marble shield
A deep-lined brow under a shouldered stone.
Phidias himself! Now they'd see him jailed
Or exiled for sacrilege, for drawing his face
On a holy monument in a public place.
O Lord of Eternity, had they but known

The monumental scale of his delight
In freeing gods from stone, not a one
That fed on envy would have abided it!
Somebody would have knifed him on the street.
Knowing the glory that was his alone,
They would not have allowed him to live on
In light or gloom, in exile or in prison.

2

Banished, he fled to Elis. The Temple of Zeus
Stood vacant there, its holy of holies
Awaiting the promised image of that God.
No man alive since Homer had his vision,
Could carve out such an idol but Phidias,
The world agreed. In taking the commission
He prayed for grace. Rumor led to legend
Rancor made the masterpiece, rancor against
His fatherland, the State of Athens
Became the medium of the Olympian Zeus;
But it was gold and ivory upon cypress,
Golden hair and beard upon ivory flesh
That gleamed in nakedness from shoulder to loins
Where golden draperies hid the divine source.

Sapphire eyes shone under a wide brow
With such compassion as no man driven
By mere lust for vengeance could portray;
Such kindness as men pray for every day,
Smiled upon eight years of this creation.
Rancor might have beaten a hand to powder
When it would not open for balancing

The winged lady, Victory. But over the years
Of dust and heartbreak, triumph and tedium,
Only sympathy with the god might succor him
Until he wondered, dreaming and waking
Who was being made and who was making
The statue, Olympian Zeus, or Phidias.
Sympathy for the god, so far from home.

3

That figure, seven times the size of man,
More vivid than a man, sat there enthroned,
Bent graciously under the sky-blue dome,
Which grazed His emerald laurel wreath.
All who entered shuddered first in terror
Zeus might rise in wrath or careless thought
And bring the sky down crashing to the floor.
Kind eyes assured the faithful He would not.
Bulls led to the altar for sacrifice,
Lions, hawks, grew gentle in that presence,
Charmed past fear. Men soul-distressed,
Heart-broken, left their pain under the eyes
Of the Guardian uniting gods and men,
The suppliant's protector. Grave misfortune
To die without ever setting eyes upon it!
All agreed. The artist conquered Hellas,
Hellas and the world, with this colossus.

4

For centuries no clear idea of God
Ruled men. Each thought of his own likeness.
Now no witness who beheld this shape
Of gold and ivory under the temple dome
Could picture Zeus in any other form.
So the high priest came to question Phidias,
His tools and methods, if the golden figure
Stood worthy in all ways of divine nature . . .

O Lord, Almighty Artist who apprenticed
Not only the youth of Elis, but all matter,
Fire, earth, and sea, wind, bird and beast,

What in the name of God could Phidias say,
Except there had never been a better sculptor,
No substance finer than gold and ivory?
Better to work up fire and earth and sea
Maybe, but who has ready tools for this?

A man can only work on what is bound
Here within water, earth and fire and wind.
O Lord of Olympia, Zeus, Supreme Artist
Who quarried pure substance, sap and soul
To make the man, the eagle, and the bull,
What could the poor sculptor tell the priest,
But that no man could be a better artist?
Let him dare compare a man with God!

Who would say that Zeus ought not be shown
In human form for fear it might please fools
To measure a mortal against God and lose
All sanctity in trade? Only a madman
Compares himself to a masterpiece like this,
In beauty, strength, insight or enormity.
And who would say no image should be made
Of God on earth, who knew the agony

Of longing to love and honor Him nearby?
We are children in exile, far from home,
Who in a waking dream reach out in darkness
For mother and father, wanting love and wisdom
No gold or stone can capture or express—
Our eyes are blind to these. There is only one
Vessel on earth that bears them, human form,
Which Phidias dared to lend to God's purpose.

Men loved the statue, hated Phidias.
Eight hundred years it sat there, long enough
To fix an image in the minds of men
So future gods in thundering power and pride
Must live or die in service of human love.
As for the man who lent the divine vision:
In Elis as in Athens he was tried
For stealing the god's gold, and died in prison.

Diana

All day you seemed fearful of me,
Your wide, brave gaze
Wavering, haunted. Then you said:
"Last night I dreamed I was a doe
And you were a country hunter with his bow
Chasing me through woods into a valley
Where your arrows would end my life."

I thought of the old story, Actaeon,
And one lesson seemed plain enough.
If you have never been in love
Like this, or thought of children
Dividing your ecstatic solitude,
You must feel like the hunter hunted,
Running from the game you have pursued.

The doe was sacred to the goddess
Of virgins, Diana, who also
Stood guardian to women in childbirth.
Actaeon, his cloak red with stag's blood
Came upon her bathing in a grotto,
Stopped and stared. The goddess then
Dashed water from the spring into his face

Saying "Go now and tell if you can
How you have seen the goddess of the chase,
Diana, without a stitch of clothing on."
And as the hunter fled
A rack of antlers sprouted on his head.
Hands turned to hoofs upon the ground,
His skin became spotted hide

And he couldn't speak to tell the hound
That first leapt for his heart
Or the hound that followed or the pack

He was their master and not a stag
To be harried, bitten, ripped apart.
I thought I'd broached a shrine of innocence
The day you took me home and I first saw

Your childhood dolls kept in a cabinet,
And the curious *milagros* on the wall:
The body torn into little silver icons,
Hand and foot, arm and heart the afflicted
Faithful hold in prayer to make them whole;
And looking down on us as we sipped tea
In your whimsical kitchen, a stuffed stag's head.

Solomon and the Four Winds

(from an ancient scroll, purportedly a reminiscence
by old Rehoboam, of his father, King Solomon)

Legends feed on legends, lies on lies,
And most of what you hear about my father
Belongs in a book of tales or fantasies,
Truth seen cockeyed, gossip unfit
For scribes to copy in the sight of God.
I would not give one line for your Chronicle
Except for a certain look about your eyes
That tells me you might write what I recall,
No more or less. Now try and set down this:

When I was young, I idolized the King
My father, studied to be like him
In every way, as good, and strong, and wise.
Coming from school late one afternoon
I saw a widow weeping on the corner,
Holding an empty bowl, wheat flour strewn
From skirt to causeway. Meaning to comfort her,
I told her take this misery to the King
And name the rascal who had spilled her flour.
Famine, war, and plagues befall the city
Where widows weep unheeded, knaves run free.

I ran home ahead of her to the palace.
This was the evening hour the royal gates
Swung open for the people's grievances.
Beggar, housewife, banker, prince, and sage
Stood in a wide circle around my father
As I approached the throne, trembling with rage.

Maybe he'd had enough of public business:
Hearing my story of the widow's sorrow,
He rapped his scepter on the marble floor
And cleared the hall.

"Where is she now?"
I told him she had followed me to court
And probably stood right outside the door.

Then what he did stunned me. He got up
And offered me his seat upon the throne,
Which suddenly seemed small in the great room
Where father and son found themselves alone.
Wrapping the robe around my narrow shoulders,
He passed the scepter, handed me his crown,
Retaining just one token of his power—
The famous ring that held dominion over
Spirits of land and fire, earth and sea.
Only once had it ever left his finger,
In a war of wits with Ashmodai,
King of demons, father lost the ring
And wandered in his kingdom for three years,
A beggar scorned, unloved, lame, and unknown.
Now in the guise of chamberlain he led
The widow through the portals to the throne
And bid her speak. She would not lift her head.

"My Lord's justice is great. And greater still
His pity for the lonely and oppressed.
As I was walking from the marketplace
Where I had spent my last shekel on flour
To bake myself a single Sabbath cake
—A roar and whistling came from the sky.
The ruffian wind came chasing after me,
Slapped a hand in my bowl and mixed my meal
With dust to twist on whirlwinds in a cloud.
Now I shall go hungry on God's sabbath
Without a coin for flour. So I cried."

Across the daring silence, father's eyes
Met mine with easy humor and a hard question:

He had given me his scepter and crown
To judge the widow's case, but kept the ring;
And no one but the man who wore the ring
Could summon those wild spirits of the air.
Without a word or nod, he knew my mind.
Bowing low in show of deference
He kissed the sky-blue sapphire on his hand,
Opened a window and called for the West wind.

I was just a boy. My father was King,
With a poet's tongue that won him love and fame.
He called upon the wind and a wind came
Blasting the valance, rippling the tapestry,
Babbling its blustery language, invisible
At first to everyone but Solomon,
Who saw and heard and fathomed everything.

He rendered up for us to see and hear
The birdlike being with long golden hair,
Wing-feathers iridescent, sparkling dew.
It bowed before the master of the ring.
And I in childish anger spoke angrily:
"You! Are you the wind that robbed the widow,
Swept her bowl of flour and left her weeping?
Admit it if you did."
                                        And the wind said:

"As I was flying over the Cyprian hills
I saw men cutting copper from the rocks.
All day and night, brown men were tunneling
Into the bare shoulder of a mountain.
When they were loaded up with the green ore
They shoveled it on coals and fanned the fire,
Till metal ran from ash like a glowing serpent.
They caught and hammered copper into plates

To cover the roof of the Temple you are building
O Solomon, on Mount Zion, in God's honor.
As for this poor woman, I've never seen her."

So Solomon let the innocent wind go free,
With a nod of his head. A second time
He kissed the sky-blue sapphire on his hand,
Opened a window, and called for the East wind.
He called upon the wind and a wind came
Blasting the valance, rippling the tapestry,
A birdlike being with long crimson hair,
Wing-feathers tawny from the desert sand.
It bowed before the master of the ring.
And I in wonder spoke out forcefully:
"You! Are you the wind that robbed the widow,
Swept her bowl of flour and left her weeping?
Admit it if you did."
The East wind said:
"As I was flying from the Abilene desert,
I circled above the mountains of Lebanon.
Down in the forest, men with iron axes
Were raising them against the ancient cedars
In whose cool crowns I love to loll and rest.
Axmen felled the trees and trimmed the branches
With iron hatchets, then with metal planes
Peeled the bark from trunks and smoothed the wood
To fashion beams for the Temple you are building
O Solomon, on Mount Zion, in God's honor.
As for this poor woman, I've never seen her."

So Solomon let the innocent wind go free
With a nod of his head.
Then a third time
He kissed the sky-blue sapphire on his hand,
Opened a window, and called for the North Wind.

He called upon the wind and a wind came
Chilling the room, whistling and sighing,
A birdlike spirit with long silvery hair,
Wing-feathers blinding bright with arctic snow.
It bowed before the master of the ring.
And I in terror spoke out valiantly:
"You, are you the wind that robbed the widow,
Swept her bowl of flour and left her weeping?
Admit it if you did."

The North Wind said:
"You summoned me from a quarry in Lydia.
There I was cooling the faces of weary men
Who toil day and night to carve white blocks
Of marble from the bowels of the mountain.
Their chisels break white marble from dark rock.
Their patient hands have chipped and smoothed
Cornerstones for the Temple you are building
O Solomon, on Mount Zion, in God's honor.
As for this poor woman, I've never seen her."

Solomon let the innocent wind go free
With a nod of his head.
A fourth time
He kissed the sky-blue sapphire on his hand,
Opened a window—in breezed the South Wind,
A spirit with auburn hair, wing-feathers red
As south-sea coral sunned under shallow wave.
It bowed before the master of the ring.
And I undoubting spoke out righteously:
"You! You are the wind that robbed the widow,
Swept her bowl of flour and left her weeping.
Admit it now."
The South Wind said: "I did—"

When with a scepter-stroke I cut him short,
Thinking at last the time had come for justice,
Though justice in what manner I knew not.
The King insisted that we hear him out.
"I am the one who did it. Hovering over
A clear sea, over the shores of Araby
I heard a clamor rise across the silence,
Voices of souls in danger crying out.
Three hundred on a ship, Egyptian peasants,
Wives and babes, in flight from drought and famine,
Had sailed for bread and shade in Araby,
And sprung a leak. Heading for the shore
They fell within a bowshot of dry land
And then green waves were swallowing the deck.
That death would overtake them on the sea
In sight of land, was such a cold torment,
Men, women and children lifted a cry
I heard before it reached the court of heaven.

I lay upon the placid sea and blew
Hard, until waves lifted their white heads.
I pushed against the sails with all my might;
The ship rose out of the surge and flew
Landward, crashed and splintered on a shoal.
Not a soul was drowned. Wading ashore
They thanked the freak wind that delivered them;
It was the same that spilled the widow's flour."

When the South Wind ceased there was a silence,
Bare as the plane tree after a hurricane, where
Thoughts like stricken birds looked for a home.

Solomon let the innocent wind go free
With a nod of his head.
He called the treasurer

And ordered him to count out ten gold coins
For the widow, led her out. He turned to me.
I had taken off the robes, the crown,
Ill-fitting marks of measureless sovereignty.
I handed him the scepter. The purple robe
He threw over his shoulder. Settling down
Upon the throne that once belonged to David,
He bid me call the crowd outside the door.
The hour was late, the world was full of troubles;
We must not keep them waiting anymore.

Jacob at Peniel

(Nightfall. Jacob rests by the ford of Jabbok
but cannot sleep.)

JACOB

Once I had no pillow but a stone
When I fled my brother's jealous wrath.
Yet I slept the night, so far from Canaan.
I bought his birthright for a cup of broth
When hunger dulled his wits. Owning that,
I slipped into my brother's robes and voice
And stole into the tent of my blind father
Who blessed me to be lord of the firstborn.
Yet I slept the night, for neither fear
Nor guilt could vex my sleep when I was young.

Twenty years have passed. God calls me home
To make my peace with Esau. So I come
To Jabbok ford and cannot sleep for fear
The rams and goats and camels I have sent
To buy his mercy will renew his spite.
And twenty years exile have worn my pride
Threadbare till it cannot hide my guilt.
What kind of God would bless me for deceit?

(The Angel approaches.)

River of stars and stars upon the river,
Stars bear witness, each one pure mind
Of fire in the mirror of the heavens.
If one star should shatter into a form
Of lights, a constellation with a face
And hands, then I might take it for a man
Striding across the river to Canaan.

ANGEL

By night the day is born, and by light, light.

JACOB

Stranger, did you come down from the sky?

ANGEL

You climbed the ladder of your questioning
To meet me in the air above the river.
I never took a step more than you did.

JACOB

I cannot sleep.

ANGEL

And I can never sleep.

JACOB

Tomorrow I must face my brother's wrath.

ANGEL

Fire upon fire, look upon my face!
For I can call no man on earth my brother.
Yet in our loneliness we may embrace.

(They meet and what begins as an embrace becomes a struggle which first the angel and at last Jacob dominates, holding the angel to the ground.)

Let me go.

JACOB

First bless me.

ANGEL

Dawn is near.

JACOB

Are you a thief that fears the light of dawn?

ANGEL

I serve the light by praising His holy name.

JACOB

Bless me.

ANGEL

I cannot give what you have won
From God the way you won it from a man.

ANGEL AND JACOB

Now we are one.

(Jacob releases the angel but
they remain joined hand in hand facing
a powerful light. The angel moves away.)

ANGEL

No more.

JACOB

I saw His face and yet I live.

ANGEL

I touched a man and yet I cannot die.
O Jacob shall be named for Israel!
Strive no more for what is yours by right.
God blesses you for your mortality.

*(The angel disappears in the
direction of the fading stars and Jacob moves
to follow but finds himself limping and pauses.)*

JACOB

By night the day is born, and by light, light . . .
Now I shall meet my brother in Canaan.

Vivaldi's Four Seasons

I. Spring

Spring is upon us, green again,
Hailed by songbirds, the west wind,
And brooks murmuring throughout the land,
Happy to leave the ice behind.

The sky goes dark. A cloud curtain
Promises thunder and lightning;
But larks will soon be returning,
Their songs refreshed by the rain.

Here on the meadow lushly grown
With wildflowers, the goatherd is sleeping,
His faithful dog dreaming nearby

While to the bagpipe's squeal and drone,
The nymphs and shepherds are dancing
Footloose, capering under a brilliant sky.

II. Summer

In the long season when the sun comes close
Men languish, cattle fade, the pines dry out.
Voice of the cuckoo is heard, then trios of
Cuckoo, nightingale, and turtledove.

Soft breezes meet a harsh wind from the north,
Hell-bent on ruin. The drowsing shepherd
Cries out of a nightmare, fearing for
The land his pillow, and his wandering herd.

Fear stirs his listless limbs, fear
Of lightning's fury under lowering skies,
And swarming pestilence of gnats and flies.

He's on his feet and running before the scorn
Of rain and thunder, his nightmare come true,
Barbarous hailstones, trampling down the corn.

III. Autumn

O peasants celebrate with song and dance
The good harvest—they love to drown
The fire of Bacchus's drink in drink until
They come to the end of joy and go lie down.

Thus the singing and dancing of each man
And woman follows the leader out of sound,
Away from the gentle music that led them on,
As autumn invites them into silent slumber.

Daybreak, the hunter comes with horn and gun,
His snarling dogs all howling at the skies.
Fox flies. Now they've got him on the run.

Once wounded, weary, frightened by the sound
Of hunter, hunter's horn and hunter's hound,
The fox, wild-eyed, runs out of hope, and dies.

IV. Winter

Shivering in snow, shivering
In the face of the cold northwester,
Stamping your feet to keep the toes
From freezing, while your teeth chatter

Makes fire and hearth more lovely
When you step in out of the weather.
Walking the frozen lake in mortal fear
At first, the rich fear of falling;

Then stepping out boldly and falling
And rising again, brave, until a cry
Of ice breaking opens a chasm and you hear

A roar through the iron gate, the invisible
War of winds, Sirocco, and cruel Boreas—
Winter joy is wrung from such bitterness.

Memorial Day

The library is closed—Memorial Day—
We honor men who died for our freedom
In wars that most of us cannot recall.
On the corner, men who should be schoolboys
Flag passing cars to deal cocaine.
The steel doors of the library are fit
For a vault. No windows figure in the wall
To let light shine on the books,
Just glass brick pocked by bullets
From drive-by shootings, thick glass
Cracked in spidery traceries
Like promises shattered. Light
From a million books burned in Berlin
Casts no shadow on the grey fortress
That is all this neighborhood will ever know
Of a library. Here the books are safe
But the readers are burning.

Helen

"Tell us a love story,"
Pleaded the class in chorus.
"Our lessons are all done,
Now don't lecture or bore us,"

They prattled, except for one,
Helen, whose gaze looked lost
In the maze of willow branches,
The girl the boys liked most

For the faraway blue of her eyes
And brown hair straight as rain.
"Tell us a love story, please,"
They begged the teacher again.

He frowned and longed for the bell,
Saying "All the love stories I know
End in heartache, or death—"
Then Helen, from the back row

Called at last from her daydream
In the voice of an innocent lover,
"Tell us a love story anyway
And stop before it is over."

From *Spirits* (1987)

for David Bergman

Cygnus Musicus

Note the scale of tones that flies from a brass bugle
and, trusting that Nature creates nothing in vain,
compare the horn's shape to the windpipe of a swan,
that snaky tube of bony rings. You see
the bird's instrument is altogether equal
to playing the music praised in antiquity:
those plaintive strains, a cello-like requiem
murmuring through the reeds its prophetic sigh
as death waves the swan toward asylum where
no one may hear him sing, no other bird
break up the sacrament of his dying hymn.

Also in the windless glow of a sea-beach
they sing before sunrise, says Oppian.
Pythagoras was so moved he began to teach
that the poet's soul in death becomes a swan
so his divine harmony will not be lost.
One night before Plato came to Socrates
the sage dreamed a swan hid in his breast;
and hours from execution the swan sounded
to him like a joyous prophecy of the Good
waiting for us there in the next kingdom,
and not some hyperbole of bestial dread.

Now it seems the swan's melodic gift is fading
or one must be dead to hear it. I have stood
long hours by lakes and estuarine rivers
and recall only a stridulous braying, though none
of my subjects was ever summoned by death,
the singing master. I will go on straining
my ears in the twilight between hope and dread
I shall catch that mythic descant of the swan,
out of my senses at last to hear the singing,
like a father who hears the voice of his lost son,
that supreme fantasia, the soul's returning.

The Bride's Profile

She cannot see her profile in the mirror,
    a blessing, the painter would insist,
the mystic Heinrich Bebie, circa 1850,
    easel propped in the entry of the bride's
chamber, chimes before the wedding. O
    not that she lacks charm! The waterfall
of veils discloses nape and arm and breast
    to overwhelm the bridegroom's fantasy.

A jewel box agape on the dresser top
    has yielded up the pearls of her trousseau.
Between the leaning bride and her mirror image,
    a boat-shaped urn of gold glows—at the bow
a sculpted cherub, at the stern, for grip,
    a tiny maid that might pass for a boy.
The sylph's head is sainted by the halo
    of the mirrored bride's camellia corsage.

Better, Bebie muses, she cannot see
    the mirror at this moment. Although
reflections are mere accidents of light,
    of life confronting life momentarily:
a girl stunned by her beauty suddenly,
    or woman by its loss, a meditative willow
drawn into a glassy stream that carries away
    its picture invisibly to be whirled and broken

among rocks and rapids, distilled in crystal spray—
    although no reflection is to be trusted,
it is better she cannot see herself in profile.
    Quite enough that I should stand and witness
the bride's profile under the chaplet of pinks,
    her milky brow, the maiden tenderness
harden in the mirror. The cruel twin yoked
    with the oblivious bride, gazing parallel,

hawk-nosed, hawk-eyed, lips galled to a line,
    glares at the bride's dream that was her doom
and curses with wedged eye a bearded man
    who haunts the faded doorway of the mirror.
When I am dead, thinks Bebie, some will wonder
    who was that weary spectre in the doorway,
lingering, too old to be the groom.
    It is the man who will give the bride away.

Champagne

All the angels that might fit
    on the head of a pin,
every spirit with its petty sin
    must pass through here
        on the way to bliss.

They appear out of nowhere
    in silver chains
rising through the clear crucible,
    and scatter in the gold
        to dance for us,

then at the crystal heights
    burst into chorus.

Raphael

1

The gallery light left something to be desired.
Electric ghosts in clouds and streaks
told their moral on the bulletproof glass:
the soul will make a mirror of any window.
I shifted. It made no difference at all.
From where I looked into the constant space
of your self-portrait, my own face
shot back at me from your burnished eye
like the floating image on a gypsy's ball.

Poor Narcissus. If he could have seen
your clear eyes spending light
as if the generous stream where lovers bend
to drink each other's images
ran to and from your vision's hidden spring;
had Narcissus seen such eyes within
the silver of the pool, he might have known
a luckier myth and lived it, loving
a face far more beautiful than his own.

Just whisper, and I will sound an echo
in the bowl of viridian hills around Urbino,
in the high-walled gunmetal streets of America.
Come live in these matchstick verses,
and leave the frail galleries of the world
where beauty wore out its welcome long ago.
One critic took an axe to the Pietá,
moved by pity to crush the Saviour's skull.
The world is a perilous museum now.

Your work survived a trial of centuries,
fire, flood, and war. "Lo Spasimo,"
the Bearing of the Cross, shipwrecked en route

to the monks of Oliveto, rode the cold
waves to the port of Genoa unscathed.
When Rome was sacked four hundred years ago
French merchants tried to burn your tapestries,
char the silk and wool threads from the gold.
Your living figures blew their torches out.
Now a mock sun threatens every city
and there's scant breath left in humanity
to blow it out. Your pictures tremble on the wall
so we can hardly see them through the glass.
Man is in love with an image of himself
that has nothing to do with beauty.
It is a mask of terror, a hunchbacked elf
hailing the Last Judgment with bitter glee.
Whisper, and make our hearts your gallery.

2

Beryl blue, the Umbrian ravine
where an old man lived in solitude,
Father Bernardo, joyful anchorite.
Barren of all but faith, he claimed two daughters:
one the oak tree shading his frail hut,
and one a singing child of the vine dressers,
Mary, who brought his dole of bread and wine.
Two daughters, one silver-tongued, one mute.

December brought a shrill and barbarous gale
that furrowed Heaven's front and swelled the cheeks
of thunderheads that rioted over the hill,
sweeping deep-rooted pines from valley glades.
After the wind and rain, what little stood
tumbled under the stampede of a flood.
When clouds parted at last for the ruffled sun,
Mary went to see where Bernardo had gone

and learned how the silent daughter had saved him.
When freshets lashed his windowsill
he shinnied up a drain to the bark shingle.
When white waves came lapping at the eaves
he looked to the starless Heaven; whereupon
oak branches bowed low, beckoning him to climb
into their arms. Safe there in the crown
he prayed for his other daughter to help him down

and home to warm his bones and feed him bread,
for the storm had almost made an end of him.
How could he repay them? Prayer was all he had.
Bernardo called upon Heaven to bless
his daughters, the silver-tongued and the speechless,
praying Time would remember them together.
Time takes the pilgrim where he aims his hymn.
Climbing the golden verses ladderwise,

Bernardo views the future: Mary wed,
the bloom-cheeked mother of two beaming sons.
The oak tree, felled, makes staves for a wine cask.
Mary rocks in the arbor, child at breast,
her tunic viridian, skirts blue berylline.
The toddler binds a cross of apple wood.
Out of a shadow strays a strange young man
rubbing his eyes as if this were a dream. It is

a dream, but what he makes of it proves real
beyond ages of human questioning.
He crayons on cracked staves of the wine cask
a breathing horizon of ripe womanhood,
circle of red-sleeved arms, head bowed to love
the pearl of a boy. O static ecstasy!
A gold-edged halo hums, lights from above
this pearl within the pearl, his grey-winged eye.

3

Even in death is no escaping
the broad joke of mortality.
Ambitious antiquarians
in 1833

had a skull they thought was yours
and nothing else would do
but dig up the floor of the Pantheon
trying to find you,

make sure you were all there,
make sure the casket was full.
They found your little skeleton
and, *mirabile dictu,* the skull!

Man's name is carved in his skull,
omo, a man, the same,
round eyes either side of the nose.
Death knows only one name.

King and Pope were summoned
to thank the Lord it was you.
Hurrah! said the crowd in Rome.
Hurrah for the glass case too

where your skeleton dangled before
you were laid in the marble tomb
to the tune of a hidden choir,
and everybody went home.

Nature feared to be conquered
while you lived. After you died
Nature feared for her life,
as if people and countryside

would fade with your vision.
The sun might sicken with grief,
flowers retire to the underworld,
the forest fall with the leaf.

The bright oculus winks above
Raphael's Pantheon tomb.
I would like to rest here with him
but there's no more dying room

on earth and little time
till Nature closes her doors
on the last of us. I will look
for my grave among the stars.

The Carpenter

Old enough to know her father's need
for sleep, she would not wake him with her cry.
Through quartered window glass the cold
rides on the moonlight flooding her room,
casting a shadow cross on the bare wall.
She would not cry although the light seems cruel

as winter, cutting through the quilts and sheet,
tightens its grip on her legs. The pain there
thrives on, though raised in the dull heat
of summer when fever with a brutal hand
yanked the legs from under her, folding them
back to kneel as if she must pray forever.

But something stirs her father. And he turns
in his own pain, wakeful, knowing her awake,
leaves his bed and climbs the narrow stair;
rising toward the moon in the window beside her,
he sees her speechless eyes and smooths her hair.
He pulls a chair up to the glass that shines

in its beveled skin of ice. A single fingernail
rough work has left intact, becomes his tool
scratching on one quarter of the pane: a flower.
His daughter smiles to see it bloom in silver
on the moonlit wall, the first of a full garden
where two lovers are walking hand in hand.

It has been years since he has known
this freedom of making, since necessity
bartered plane and chisel for his pen.
He moves on to the second pane, a woman rocking
a child, its curled hand reaching for her lips,
her hair bound in a low hive but for a strand.

His daughter's eyes are moon-wide now, yet calm,
eager for the next image. His cold hand
etches on the third pane a fine rose window
and altar rail where a young woman is kneeling,
her dress and petticoats ruffled like a peony,
under the priest's blessing, her first communion.

Smiling, she nods. One pane is frosted blind.
He cannot think to move his hand, it moves
as her eyes close, rescued from this vision:
he draws a hill and road that winds behind
where men and women vanish two by two,
climbing in slow procession, following, what?

The sudden heat of breath and hands has made
a rainstorm on the landscape—his work is done.
He kisses her asleep. On the stray fringe
of frozen light from the golden mural, he gropes
his way downstairs, thanking the full moon,
knowing the sun will never be so kind.

Thinking of Thomas Moore

A book that I knew only by the cover,
climbed to a high shelf on a crumbling ramp
years ago, the relic of an old affair.
I took it down, hoping to find out
how one famous bard ran out of fame
and why he had come to haunt me suddenly.
I cracked the book. There was his Irish pout
engraved on the flyleaf, a spiteful genie
whose gratitude grew bitter in the lamp.

The curl of his lip, the eye's tenacity,
show us Tom Moore was not prepared to die,
at least not in print. A preface tells
his life. Born in Dublin, a grocer's son,
he studied with the tutor of Sheridan,
at fourteen enrolled at Trinity,
wrote the sensational "Odes of Anacreon"
that made him a star before the age of twenty.
Small of stature, "though in wit a man,"

he never grew up. But he sold more
poems than anyone but Byron who
called them "leadless pistols" in a satire.
Moore sent the modern Juvenal a challenge
then recalled it. They became fast friends.
When Byron died, he left Moore as legacy
his *Memoirs* to transmute to pounds
in the crucible of public curiosity.
Tom committed them to a gentler fire.

London was shocked by his arrogance,
lack of gratitude or its excess, met
by heroic friendship or its opposite.
For scandal dines as heartily on silence
as on the juiciest gossip where

the subject is a free beauty or handsome poet.
The top blew off the kettle of conjecture.
His *Memoirs* might have served Byron's defense;
the fire branded him as a demon, sure.

But Byron has all the world to tell his story.
Moore has, at the moment, only me.
What about his poems, are there any
lost treasures under the waterfall
of foxed and fading pages, a fire opal
shaken from the crown of a classic beauty,
or merry trinket kicked from a dancer's ankle,
that rolled away flashing out of the world's sight?
I turn the pages out of a sense of duty.

There are the Irish melodies sung in the twilight
of parlors by deep-bosomed ladies and old men.
There are the chiseled "Odes of Anacreon"
in praise of deep drinking and shallow passion.
And page after page, until my eyes are sore,
love poems, love poems by Thomas Moore.
You'd think that little else was worth his time,
or worse, that there was nothing easier
than falling in love and then making it rhyme.

Whom did you love, Tom? What maid or whore
escaped your manicured verses? There's no sign
of struggle, not a curl or petticoat out of place,
nor desire that puts conscience on the rack.
Your ladies flirt and sigh. They don't talk back.
Oh world of harps and blushes, plumes and lace,
you remember the name of love but not the face.
What did you feel when the last one slammed the door
and how could you tell her from the one before?

Meanwhile a strong wind has attacked the casement
in Tom's defense, breaking up my irreverent
thoughts with louder thoughts that sound like wind
holding forth in the chimney, shaking the door
and drumming up the thunder for a storm.
Wind like thoughts, then wind in human form.
It is the furious ghost of Thomas Moore
rather dignified by death, or by the lightning.
"Who are you to disturb me in oblivion?"

"It's quiet here but I've gotten used to it
now that my friends are dead and I've stopped waiting
to be rediscovered. There's a worse thing
than being forgotten: false laurel, early fame
borrowed from an ancient poet's name.
I paid for that. And I paid for my height
in love affairs that never made a rhyme,
their pain was so much greater than my art.
Honor this pure silence, and mind your own heart."

The Date

Just as you were about to step out
in your sleek, black-sequined dress
fresh from the second-hand store, veteran chic
as only a fifty-year-old dress knows how to be—

just as you pulled the shades down by the ring
and shut the door, as you were walking
toward night and the rest of your life,
a lover, a quiet place where you might find one—

just as you stopped for the passing car
that braked so the boys could whistle as
you kicked back your leg, looked over your shoulder
to check if the stocking seam had run askew—

just as you passed outside the bar I saw you
as you saw yourself in the turtle-shell compact,
making sure it was the same you as left home—
just then you thought of my words, felt warm inside—

and now you must stay with me forever.

Lateness

Because the past cannot bear to part with her
the present suffers. So we wait
in a lobby under the eyes of chandeliers,
in train stations, on a street corner,
and at midnight in the graveyard with a spirit
who waited in this world and waits in the next,

for her October hair and bright May skin
have taken since the beginning of earthly time
and will take forever. Time goes with her;
wherever she stops the moments turn and spin.
Little minutes are doves eating out of her hand—
but when the hours call, she does not answer.

Because her worth is beyond question or value,
kings have died for her and worlds collided,
skies caved in and hills leapt in the blue.
Her touch can melt the icecaps, make
buttercups flash in the desert, and wild daisies.
Poets have climbed to Heaven, singing her praises.

It isn't for spite she keeps you waiting there
at the small end of night's telescope. No,
it's not to belittle you with your bruised corsage
and trail of crushed cigarettes, left behind,
your shadow of beard, the useless theater tickets.
You are probably the farthest thing from her mind.

Maybe a street singer took her by surprise, or
the pattern of a scarf, scarlet and pearl-grey
made her pause and muse in the window, then
the moon would not let her go until it passed.
Maybe later in the street, admiring children
circled her on skates and led her away

laughing, into a wide park where it seems
her gentle protests failed as she tried on
their silver wheels and showed them whirling figures
they had seen before only in dreams.
Because of this, and the endless flattery of twilight,
the gay breeze beneath the sad story of each star,

she must honor the times that make her beautiful.
And the wonder is not that she is late tonight
but that anyone has ever seen her at all.

The Glass

Arc of flying horses, lily fan,
earth-rooted seeds that flower in the brain,
and now this woman
with all the tricks of nature to multiply
leaf upon leaf and heartbeat upon beat,
has come to live in my mind, as if
the world were not wide enough to hold her beauty.

I see her every hour of the day.
Nights are not long enough, nor the halls
of dreams where we pass on the way
to the radiant memory of passing.
Darkness is not enough, the single gift
the underworld provides us while we live,
to serve as a background for fantasy.

Restless with nights and dreams
she has to stand
up white as a diamond lightning struck
in broad daylight, between me and the world.
When she walks into the room something must break,
mind's image meets her coming with such force.
My glass is shattered and I cannot speak.

Pas de Deux

Plucked from the night above that tivoli
    of amber strung zigzag along the shore
I feel like I have been picked up and thrown
    from blizzard to the tropics, door to door.
The wall of heat; palm trees in sulphur light,
    my name on a sign held by a stranger-host
who smiles like he has known me all my life;
    two ward-heelers, three-odd journalists,

briefcase, baggage, my flight-stunned guitar
    crowd a limousine to the Grand Hotel
where the night clerk begs my signature
    in trade for a folded note. My gilded key
rings on marble as I read her name,
    phone numbers: "Welcome. Call if you have time."
Faster than thought the chandelier cascades
    and columns sway, my footmen turn to mice,

the lobby spins, a giant clockface flies
    cartoonlike behind the night clerk's back.
Faster than light, time hurls me into the dark
    room in Bristol ten years ago, and
Botticelli's cherub, all lips and eyes
    above and imponderable roundnesses below,
our bed under skylight next to the window
    sailing to ecstasy on a surge of stars.

Strangers, two embraced until one cried
    we knew each other better than ourselves,
the lover's dream, or lie that has come true,
    the touchstone: such a brilliance I have tried
to measure by it every new caress,
    the cataclysms of my mind and blood,
judge joy and sorrow by that vividness,
    which still assuages pain, humbles delight.

Ten years ago I left a girl in Bristol
        wondering would I ever see her again,
thought best to forget her, and could not.
        The girl became a woman whose beauty grew
fantastic as hope of finding her ran out
        and passing time said this is just desire's
handiwork, vain Galatea, unanswered prayer.
        Maybe this prodigy exists nowhere.

But I am to meet a dancer of the same name,
        famous here. Could she be the beauty
I recall? And even if she is,
        what made the power of that memory?
I watch the doorman's eyes for any sign
        of wonder flashing through revolving glass . . .
at last it comes, his wooden countenance
        is branded as she enters, blinding the space

and all heads turn to notice, then to stare.
        One mystery gone: she wears the face I dreamed.
Yet this would be simple, as any miracle
        is simple, only strange because it happens.
A saint stands in the flame yet will not burn,
        the statue weeps, the water runs to wine;
simple things, the flame, the wine, the tears,
        yielding a mythic beauty in ten years.

So much for the lesser mystery, the great one
        hides within it like a Chinese box
as we turn to face each other on a couch
        and twilight closes around the cornered hour.
What made the memory? Beauty alone
        fades quickly in the mind and leaves no trace.
Was I like a silly goose awakening then
        from a second birth, and imprinted upon

the first bright thing I saw, which was her face?
    If so, it might have been most anyone.
She listens, reticent as I explain
    my silence, that began so long ago.
She hears me, and eyes of beryl begin to glow
    and glisten as I pause, begin again
in the dwindling hour that must contain ten years
    or crack like crystal brimming with liquid fire,

and now reminds me she is the one who called
    though I am the one to blame for getting lost.
"And I have struggled with a coeval ghost
    or angel, in rooms of mirrors, stage after stage,
New York to Paris, ghost with eyes of living stone
    that monitored each arabesque and spin . . ."
whose fury for perfection would have thrown
    the body and spirit of a lesser woman.

And she has come to see these eyes of mine
    read in the faint lines of her hands and brow
that courage held her ten years in my mind
    as in the world. It was not her beauty alone.

Homage to Mallarmé

1. The Barrel Organ

Since my Vivian left me
to fly to another star—
Orion was it, Altair,
or the pale emerald, Venus?
—I have loved being alone.

All day I sit alone, but
for the cat, and one poet
of the Latin decadence.
Since my woman has gone
I love the legends of autumn:

slow days of September,
autumn's prologue, the hour
the sun rests before it goes,
when rays copper the walls
and redden the windowpanes;

the slowly fading echoes
of the last hours of Rome,
those languid poems that come
before Barbarian cries
and stammering Christian prose.

I was deep in one of those
I love, whose patches of rouge
thrill me more than the rose
flesh of a budding girl, and
plunging an idle finger

into the cat's black fur
I heard, outside my window
the melancholy singing
of a barrel organ. Under
the tree whose leaves in spring

seem dreary since Vivian
passed by for the last time,
I heard the sorrowful engine
that turns dreams to despair.
Then I heard it murmuring

some cheerful, vulgar reprise
that once made the back streets gay.
Yet the tune reached into my soul
and called the tears to my eyes
as no ballad has ever done.

I sipped at that song like wine
and would not go to the window
to send down my coin ringing
for fear I might see the organ
was not alone in its singing.

2. The Water Lilies

That flaming July I had gone
searching for water lilies and the friend of a friend's
estate. Gliding along the reflection
of a double landscape, rowing through both I ran aground on
this clump of reeds in midstream, my dawn voyage ending
in mystery
where the stream swelled to a fluvial thicket, and a pond
wrinkled though unconcerned
by the indecisions of its spring.

Closer inspection revealed this
green barrier in the current concealed a low arch
of a bridge that flowed into shrubbery,
enclosing lawns. I understood. This was the park of Madame

X, the unknown chatelaine I had come to call upon.
The nature of
a lady who would seek out a retreat so damply im-
penetrable must be
to my liking. Surely she had made

an inner mirror of crystal
shielded from the glaring indiscretion of her days
and when she appeared the silver willows,
leaf by leaf, would shimmer in the limpidity of her gaze.
Bent as if under a vast weight before the stranger
would come to speak
I smiled at my easy enthrallment to the feminine
possibility, that
I might be enchanted by anyone.

Then a sound, scarce audible, made
me wonder if that lady would divide my leisure, or
hope against hope, was it the stirring pool?
The footfall ceased. O subtle secret of steps that begin and fade
leading the mind here and there as they wish, aswirl in
petticoat lace
flowing as if to surround the will in a watermark
by which she makes her way
heel and toe under sweeping brocade!

Does she know why she paused? Is it
to keep these reeds and my mind's drowsiness between us
veiling lucidity, holding above
my head the very mystery that confounds me? "O lady,
to whatever ideal your features conform, I fear
their precision
would ruin my deepest pleasure in the rustling of your
arrival, a certain
charm defenseless against invasion."

Separated, we are one. I
mingle with her in strange intimacy, in this sublime
suspense afloat where my dreaming delays
this hesitant lady more than any number of suitors
could do. How many idle speeches would it require
to discover
so intuitive an agreement as I contrived in
order not to be heard?
Now my will rests on the scales of time . . .

O my dream, tell me what to do,
render in a glance that virgin space in solitude
as in memory of this place I pluck
one of those magic water lilies that suddenly rise up
enclosing with hollow whiteness a perfect absence
made of new dreams,
of the joy that will never be and my breath held in fear
of an apparition.
I leave with one, rowing in silence

slowly, so not to break the spell
in my flight by casting a ripple toward the shore
where anyone coming might discover
in foam or bubble a clear simile for the abduction
of my ideal flower. Yet if the lady comes, drawn by
apprehension
something strange has occurred, if the lady, that wild, proud, or
thoughtful lady should come,
so much the worse for the ineffable

face I shall never know! I pushed
off and was skirting a bend in the stream homeward bound,
bearing away my fictitious treasure
like some glorious swan's egg from which no flight will ever spring,

swollen with nothing more than that emptiness of pure
self, exquisite,
a lady pursues down paths of a tidal garden, pausing
now and then on the edge
of a spring to be crossed, or a sound.

3. Old Times

Spiderwebs on the casement,
the wardrobe is ancient too,
fading curtains, peeling chairs,
nothing you own is new.

Didn't you wish, my sister,
with a glance at time vanishing,
my poems might set in meter
"the grace of some fading thing?"

New objects displease us
and scare us with their cries;
their need to be worn out
taxes our energies.

Come close that German almanac,
the days it proclaims are dead.
Lie down on the threadbare carpet,
calm child, pillow my head

on your knees in that faded gown
and I will talk on and on
of old clocks and cracked furniture
till the fields and streets are gone

under the cold of night.
Are your thoughts wandering?
On top of the casement
spiderwebs are shivering.

The Rivals

Happiness, in the fairy tale, comes hobbling
disguised as a hag. And the prince takes pity
on her, bringing her to bed, not knowing this

is happiness, thinking this is just a hag who
for some moral he values beyond comprehension
has made this trial of his magnanimity,

and no sooner does he embrace her than she
becomes an exquisite young maiden
with no past and no future apart from his.

So a man I thought my enemy came to haunt me,
featureless at first, in the dusk of dreams,
then turning slowly toward the daylight

until at last, in profile, I recognized
my old rival. He will have his revenge,
I thought, sending that face, more hideous

than anything of nature's cruel devising,
to flame up in a wall of sleepless rage
between me and all that I must see to do.

And my God, I thought, this is like love
who taught me her lesson years ago, though
she was beautiful and this is a death's head.

My enemy came to haunt me, tirelessly
until, desperate, I kissed him, kissed him
dead. Then he slept, long and beautifully.

The Testament of Isaac Lakedion

> Here is a Man come to this City,
> if he may be called a Man, who pretends to
> have lived about these Sixteen Hundred Years.
> They call him the Wandering Jew. I tell thee
> Sage Sheik, if this Man's Pretences be true,
> he is so full of choice Memoirs, and has been
> Witness to so many grand Transactions for the
> Space of Sixteen Centuries of Years, That he
> may not unfitly be called, A Living Chronology,
> the Proto-Notary of the Christian Hegira, or
> Principal Recorder of that which they esteem
> the Last Epocha of the World's duration.
>
> —*Letters Writ by a Turkish Spy*, 1686

April 22, 1984

Here in a circle of light your sleepless guest
parcels his means to pay for the night's rest.
This copper coin that might have brought me wine
or bread in Gaza when I was a boy,
bargains for an atom of your faith.
Heads: Jupiter; tails: the Pharaoh's sign,
an eagle clutching the brace of thunderbolts.
Legend claims the pouch I pluck it from
breeds a new coin when the last is gone
and so it costs me no more than these words.
But do not judge these gifts by what I own
or think I dream to match your kindnesses.
You climbed that skeleton of broken stairs
in Lloyd Street's ruined temple, to be alone,
and saw my breath rise ghostlike, leading to
this heap of rags and bones under the dome
where I chanted Kaddish for company
until I seemed to lie among the dead.
Pity conquered fear, you brought me home.

Here you bathed me, served up bread and wine
while your daughter stared at my long beard
and blushed at the sly wink of my sunken eye.
Your wife smiled as the boy hid in her dress.
We stayed up long after they went to bed,
talking of Truth and Justice in your study.
Yet I could not tell you what I would
for fear you would lose faith in me, or worse,
believe my words and never trust yourself.
So I spoke of the Parthenon before the gods
burned it behind them like a bridge.
I told of Nero's dining hall wainscoted
with pivoting ivory tiles that could transform
green mountains on the wall to a seastorm,
and flowers of gems, more true to life than life.
I wanted you to see Jerusalem
before the earthquake tore the marble veil:
how terrace upon terrace the temple rose,
with towers of gold, and colonnaded porches . . .

Then came your question floating on a whisper:
"Isaac, I am a strange Jew fallen
among kind Christians. First my mother
then my wife, now maybe my children too.
Tell me, Lakedion, who was the Christ?"
My heart, were it not cursed to run as long
as that sun pounding at the source of all,
had stopped then, but called me up the stair.
Climbing with the dead weight of that silence
composed of ancient grief and newborn fear
you might mistake my history for myth,
I longed to outrage the whole bookshelf
but did not answer. If I were a scholar
with Josephus and Plutarch at my side;
if I were a bold philosopher

with no wage but the Truth, no roof but sky,
poet or madman, I would have tried.
I have been all of these. Now I am nothing
but what I feared, a man who cannot die,
yet owns the power to unspeak himself
in one rhapsody of heedless eloquence—
as if a man of chalk should seize the cloth
and dust away his figure line by line.

Who was the Christ, who is Lakedion?
Finding the bed tenderly turned down
for one who has not slept in a star's age,
I ransacked the drawers for paper and pen,
the coward's weapon and the hero's toy.
The letter may bear what seems too strange for speech.

* * *

By Caesar's temple where the market crept
upon apothecaries' laden carts
I spun through diagonals of light,
holding my jaw that rang with toothache,
haggling over a little mandragora.
The smile that shone before him in those days,
like a cracked lantern, I felt before I saw
the lanky deep-eyed youth whose face seemed
patched from odds and ends of ancient faces.
A long nose here, a leaping eyebrow there,
held together by the smile that said:
"Though a stranger to Alexandria, I
would pit your brave toothache against the worst,
and guess it will laugh outright at mandragora."

He shrugged the goat-hair cloak that students wore.
I said, "I was born here twenty years ago
but never have I heard such insolence,"

then I danced a bit as the tooth sang,
charging him to cite some authority.
Poured forth a catalogue of witnesses
from Baccheius to Philinus of Cos,
to make me lose all faith in mandragora.
The stranger picked out catmint and staghorn
then led me north along the Canobic Way
past the soma where Alexander lay
fresh in his honey-filled coffin of glass,
past tomb and temple, gardens and more tombs.
He said it must be easy to die here
where the living live among the dead.
And I gaped, for as if summoned by the thought,
two Mareotic mystics glided by
whose cosmic eyes intrigued my visitor
although I warned their cult was under ban.

This Jeshua Ben Joseph, Nazarene,
came from Jerusalem the long way round
via Babylonia and Thebes,
consulting Chaldee mage and Coptic priest
upon the marriage of the flesh and soul.
Now he would study healing and Greek thought
in this attic perched high in the Jewish Quarter.
He bid me stretch out on a mat of reeds
and pounded up a pomegranate rind
with poppy juice and smeared some on my gum
while he was fomenting the foul poultice.
This Jeshua Ben Joseph was renowned
for undoing Hillel's legendary patience,
by vaunting a preternatural memory
of scripture, and mocking the Sabbath law.
He told me: After hearing the schools debate
whether the wife might dress in head-bangle
or golden tiara shaped like Jerusalem,

whether the lame should go out on a crutch,
horse with chain or Libyan ass with bridle;
after yawning through days of such disputation,
he heard the masters litigate the roebuck.
"A sin," they all agreed, "to hunt the deer
on Sabbath. But suppose a stag leaps through
the doorway, might a good man slam it shut?"
Jeshua called from the gallery: "Rabbi,
if the house had no more room than yours
one would be foolish not to shut the doors;
that buck might be the leader of his herd,
and one deer in the house on Sabbath is plenty.
Rabbi, would Moses whittle such a pipe?
Is the world a ring for angels and demons
to fight for souls according to our rules?"

Said Hillel: "*Man* inflamed the jealousy
of angels the double-winged Sammael led,
and made those demons. Evil is man's burden.
But God gives us the law to learn and serve.
Study, Jeshua, and peace await thee."
Peace might wait, but Jeshua would not:
"You so clutter man's pathway with your law,
he stumbles if he does not sit at home
like you, sifting husks for grains of truth
while naked children beg outside the door.
Study Goodness Itself a little while,
lift the latch, and feed and dress the poor!"
Now Hillel, famed for charity, cried out:
"Go! Seek the hour that is not night or day
and there, there you may study Goodness Itself."
So Jeshua had come down from Jerusalem.

I slept. When I awoke the pain was gone.
I hailed a miracle. He called it science,

mastery of the numbers and the will.
How might I pay him? He asked if I knew
the Jewish Greeks (he called them Greekish Jews)
who read the Pentateuch in the full glare
of Pagan wisdom. So he came to me
when he could steal away from Medicine,
to share my desk and scrolls in the Atheneum.

That was spring. By harvest, the man
had plucked up Plato by his roots,
which proved to be the locks of Moses' hair.
Then, up leapt the Patriarch himself
from Genesis and Exodus to show
his words were manna to the Greeks, their words
bent rays refracted from the purest light.
We saw creation's God as architect
who bears in mind the blueprint of a town
before his thought takes on timber and stone.
Man in God's image summoned a man of dust
and a supercelestial constellation
gave to sun and stars their natural light,
while real trees sprung from His seedless forest.
The Psalmist sang our method, word for word:
"Thus spake the Lord, twofold was what I heard."
We did unfold the wrinkled Pentateuch
till it lay smooth and bright as the rolled silver
heralds use to flash from peak to peak.

Jeshua raised his eyes from Exodus.
"So, Isaac, Moses knows the world's a bubble,
which I mean to prove to Hillel by and by."
I asked him what that meant, and he replied:
"The laurel tree outside the Atheneum,
that giant, rooted south of the portico?
Look for it there next time you go by."

The sun behind him made me wink or doze,
next thing I knew was twilight, he was gone.
Sunup, I hurried to the Atheneum
and what! It seems the land had wheeled around.
The laurel tree whose limbs I knew by heart,
though every leaf and bird nest was in place,
had leapt from south to north of the portico,
leaving no speck of earth nor a spade's trace.
I fumed in the open green, so recently
filled with laurel in my memory.
I'd grown up in a world of brazen mages
who could speak doves and paint the air with ships;
I'd seen them raise the dead who'd gladly then
die once more to be brought round again
in Soter's name, or Kore's or Cybele's.
So when he strolled across the garden smiling
I said I had no eyes for miracles.
We were still Jews and enemies to sham,
for life is baffling enough a miracle
and magic grossly *contra naturam.*

"But Moses," said Jeshua, "did he not turn
his stick into a snake, the Nile to blood?"
"When Moses does those tricks it's literature,"
I said, "with you I fear it's truth itself,
your vivid thoughts trespassing on the world.
If you can do it so might anyone
and life would fan into a million visions
where not a tree or mountain would be safe."

He said this was his lesson, and a Jew
might work a miracle to teach the truth
though not for profit. Would I have him move
the laurel where it pleased my memory?
We laughed, and left it for philosophy,
where for a little while things might stand still.

There lay the arena of our second quarrel.
The sun led our way to the study room.
I said the sun was bright in the South room,
which meant to me the room was full of light.
But Plato had crowned the heaven of our thoughts
with such a sun as beat by day and night,
which was God's image, though by no means God,
the hidden, sourceless fountain of everything.
Moses knew, who saw the burning bush.
We talked across a table sun-bleached white
and he said maybe God was in the room,
which meant to me Creation, like sunlight
that springs from the sun and yet is not the sun.
And so I said "Creation dwells among us."
We sat hushed, wondering by what art
the Unseen, dwelling inexorably apart,
had made the room and two of us talking there.
At last, he whispered "words" which meant to me
words but what he really meant was reason,
the spin of thoughts in mind before you talk.
God thinks and a flower blooms like speech;
He thinks the law and Moses writes it down.
I thought of the voice behind the cherubim
above the golden cover of the Ark,
a Voice above the ladder in Jacob's dream,
thunder on Sinai, words flashed in the dark.
All our thinking led us to this pass:
the world is like nothing so much as speech
streaming daylight from an unknown Sun.
And our Creator's powers and his grace
speak in rare moments to godlike men.
"So, Isaac," he said, "God is in the room,
the son of man as he was meant to be,
His powers dressed in flesh and words and light."
I looked at the floor, the roof beams, then at him

and said: "I am not Moses, nor are you.
I'd sooner face the real sun in this room
than think you believe that to be true."
"Isaac," he said, "are you not a word of God?
And speaking now, could you not speak for Him?
Are we not, the two of us, a phrase
from the sentence passed upon our world,
uttered in perfect wisdom and boundless love?"
I told him he might be, but I was not.
Moses might be such a suppliant Word,
his thoughts divining the way of natural laws,
but Moses lived in a book.
                                        As for me
it had been enough to say grass grows,
there's good in man, and God is merciful.
That any breathing man might claim to be
the Word that speaks creation into being,
was madness, death-defying blasphemy.

* * *

That winter Cholera made port in our town
and Jeshua left my study to heal the poor.
They kept him days in a slum until the fire
he'd quelled for so many, turned upon him.
I fed the oil lamp beside his bed
and sponged him as he raved, delirious,
of men who'd begged him to dash out their brains
while others pledged their souls to marble gods.
He'd seen a baby crying at the breast
of a girl whose moon-wide eyes stared at the sun,
the ring fingers cut from both her hands.
He begged me check the ashes he had strewn
for prints of the cockfooted Shedim, a demon
he said would come before the Angel of Death.
No footprints but mine, as I bore the jars

of potion that ran through him as through a sack,
soaking the blankets that he rolled upon.
Three days it took the drug to calk his belly.
Then he rose and ate a little bread.
I said I missed him at the Atheneum
for we had many a verse to riddle out
of Ezra, Malachi, and furious Nahum.
Yet even as he smiled I was afraid
he'd leapt somewhere I could not follow him.
And finally he whispered, "I know nothing,"
with a dull sadness, brother to despair.

By Mareotis Lake, men studied death,
were schooled in ancient Thracian mysteries
and lived ideas we scarcely dared to speak.
"Isaac, all our learning is a cipher
if we cannot teach a man to die.
Let us go now where they study death."
I told him life was text enough for me.
Besides, our law condemns their secrecy.
"They know something, Isaac. Look into their eyes.
They know something. What is it they know?"
I told him no one knew just what they knew
though rumors had been ripening for years.
Some returned, as true to their silence
as others who were never seen again,
said to be honored in sanctum sanctorum
as constant guardians of the mystery.
Darkness that terrified me drew him on.
Pomegranates flashed by the Southern Gate
their scarlet blooms against the pale fig trees—
no sooner was he hale than he was gone.

I do not want to know what he saw there.
Once in a low tavern when I was young

I heard a greybeard scream at the deaf air
his eyes had seen Zagreus divided,
that this was the hand that reached into his side
and held the live heart beating above his head.
He still felt it pulsing on his tongue
and blood he'd swallowed would not let him die.
Hands out of a shadow silenced him.
I do not want to learn what he learned there
or in Memphis, Antioch, and Rome
thereafter, as he gained such mastery
it made the tricks and thoughts he played on me
look like a boy's strength against a man's.

* * *

I did not see my friend for seven years.
I had gone up to Jerusalem,
my studies having won me at long last
preferment in the Coptic embassy
to the Court of Herod.
                                        I began to hear
wild rumors of this Jew in Capernaum.
Fearing neither God nor the Sanhedrin
he'd raised so many dead and dying men,
he had to work more miracles to feed them
and spoke such truth the thunder stopped to listen.
So after the first riot in the Temple
when he was summoned to the magistrate
and scolded, I met him as he went out.
His face had come together, but the smile
was gone. Now he was sad and beautiful.
He kissed me. We walked by the pool of Siloam.
I asked him if he knew what he was doing
and he said he had come to proclaim Heaven.
I laughed, and then I wished that I were dead.
"Isaac, you have not seen how men suffer

for want of bread we broke in paradise
years ago in our sunlit world of thought.
I teach, I heal, but many cannot learn
and Heaven must shed mercy on everyone—"
"Teach on," I cried, "for there is nothing else.
Heal, but leave the miracles to God,
leave God to God and learn humility.
Each life is its own struggle to make a soul.
You cannot haul us back to paradise,
man, woman, cripple, saint, and fool
without voiding the world of everything
but you, in one sunburst of godliness
to make yours the one battle against evil."

His answer came to me before his voice
and I wept for the certainty that he was mad
and doomed, and I turned from him as he said:
"I am His Word, Isaac, and they shall eat
of my body who can never touch my thought."

I turned away. He went back to Capernaum
while I, from a whispering aerie of the Court,
heard plots to get him for treason and heresy.
They showed him the mason's withered hand,
dared him to heal it on the Sabbath day.
Jeshua sadly bid the man extend
the pallid claw, which then commenced to throb
and burst full as the flower of any hand.
My coded missives warned him against this.
I could not stop his feeding the four thousand
or healing leper, mute, and lunatic
who babbled, howled and grimaced, limped to him.
By secret letter, courier, and prayer
I told him to stay out of Jerusalem.
But he came, reining the wild colt over palms
and cloaks on the caravan road from Jericho,

weeping amid the chorus of hosannas.
I could not reach the temple for the crowds
jostling to hear him muzzle the Pharisees
who schemed to tangle him in a skein of words.
He fought with speech, they thought with clubs and swords.
I would have said: Get out of Jerusalem.
Those men you shame
are marking you for sacrifice to Caesar
while Herod yawns and Pilate quails
at Procula's dream and quits the judge's chair.
And most, who do not love you, will not care.

Three stars arose, three silver trumpets called
eager pilgrims to the Pascal Feast
while I ran through town from door to door,
wild-eyed Elijah seeking the hidden guest.
Though he was everywhere I could not find him.
So I prayed the hour would pass away
and passed mine in a pothouse with green wine.
Signum bibendi calicis. The cup
would not pass away, sweat mingled with blood
fell in heavy beads on the garden ground.
Thunder of horses, lightning of torch on stave,
ranks of the tribunes slammed and held him bound.
While I lay dreamless on the reeking board
a living nightmare rose and stalked the town.
They led him on a leash from Priest to King,
sped by whip-thong laced with spike and bone,
Praetorium to Palace and back again
till the white robe Herod lent to make him clown
king shone royal purple from the stain
that rose from whip strokes, dripped from his thorn crown.
While I lay in a tavern on the road
to Calvary they braced him with the cross.
I woke to prying light, a dull roar like
the savage surf of shouts a fighter hears

waking from the blow that deadened him.
Hiding my eyes, I stumbled to the door.
Under the sun I saw the spreading crowd
drawn by a man bent double under his load
as if he were hauling them on a wide sled.
And such a roar quaked heaven's one-eyed skull,
boomed from their hearts and tongues, a heathen cry,
a chord I'd known only as separate notes,
as laughter, pity, rage, the mad sublime
diapason of humanity
sang at once on earth for the first time.

They sang for him. He hauled them along
the road to Calvary where I stood by
cursing the pride and rank stupidity
of the wisest man that I had ever known.
I wanted to hit him. I wanted to hide
but stood my ground under the tavern sign
where he stopped to rest and look me in the eye.
Thinking my voice lost in the general cry,
I whispered, knowing his love, feeling his pain:
"You would not rest before. So now be gone."
But all the earth stood silent as he said:
"I'm going. You'll stay till I come again."

I thought he'd turned my trembling flesh to stone.
The crowd closed in behind him, they vanished
over the hill. I stood dead still, alone.
I did not move until his great heart burst
firing above the cross a second sun
that would not keep its zenith but bent down
burning to spirit all it breathed upon
and taking away the light that had been given.
I ran for the Temple. Did he not
once say that he had come to set

fire to the world? Would this bring Heaven?
What is the future but some prophet's will?
I ran as earthquakes opened grave and tomb
and heard the rending of the Temple Veil.

I thought I would die of fright. And forty years
later when the Temple melted down
as prophets of all nations had foretold,
I thought I would die of grief, and I was old.
Counting my heartbeats in a pauper's room
with a fading view of Pharos and the sea,
the first time I became a boy again
I thought it was a trick of memory
at death's door, a brief reprieve of vision.
I looked for my father's house. It was gone
from the ruined street I'd paced as an old man
where now I walked in youth and was unknown.
I held my ancient heart in a boy's hand
and wandered from Alexandria to Rome,
Paris, London, a stranger to every land.
O you that have loved and lost, living to mourn
the passing of some longed-for loveliness,
stretch your grief upon some twenty lives
to know the anguish of my memories.
You that have known the high tide of suffering
and watched your child precede you into death,
I have outlived my children's children's child
and known such loneliness I cannot bear
to look at any scene that I have loved
or bid a cherished face goodbye again.
O you that bloom and fade, bright butterfly
of summer, can't conceive my solitude.
Who was he to deny my right to die?
Was it for spite? No, no, he loved me
and maybe hoped I'd have the strength to live

as witness to the truth of history
and guard against mankind's oblivion.
He said I would stay here till he returns.

Well enough. I have learned to love the world.
It's not so difficult in this morning light
of April when pear blossoms jeweled in dew
spin from glossy branches to the grass.
It's not so difficult in your new house
where I am welcome, blesséd and can bless.
Living, I have learned to love the world
and with my vision of the consequence
I would as soon he would not come again.

When you read this letter I shall be gone.
Daylight fills the caverns of the moon
and I feel that green tingling that comes before
a new life! Whoever lived so long as I
without being born over and over again?
I'll cast off this rough and mottled skin,
my scribbled face, my cataract of whiskers
when the new moon winks her crescent eye.

I leave this coin, that might have bought me wine
or bread in Gaza when I was a boy,
to bargain for an atom of your faith.
Some say the leather pouch I pluck it from
breeds a new penny when the last is gone
and so it is mine forever, like my life:
the more I live the more I am forgiven,
my heart cannot be emptied, nor quite filled.
Do not judge my gift by what I own
or think I dare to match your kindnesses.
The coin is copper but the words are gold
as a rose some lover dreamed, and waking held.

The American White Pelican

Calmly afloat some distance from the shore, the pelican
has been taken for a sail,
its moist feathers glistening in sunlight.
A large flock flying is a seraphic sight, wings beating
in unison, apparently
without effort. After a few strokes they coast
in faultless arcs, often at miraculous height.

Honeycombed with air cells, they cannot plunge from the wing.
But the orange skin hanging
from its bill may be stretched in the service
of gluttony, driving the small fry into shallows
as they arrive with the new tide
to prey upon flies and gnats caught in the rise
and lower life swirled in the drift washing seaward,

the great fish schooled to shadow the small, eagerly
heedful of taking life in
order to sustain it. All seabirds know this
and the time of its coming. Now the white pelicans
that have been patient in a line
along the beach, steal into the surf, then
so not to fright lugworm or gudgeon, smoothly glide out.

Some distance from land they scud into line in stern accordance
with the sinuosity
of the beach, facing shoreward awaiting
their leader's motive. Then all is commotion: the birds
flailing the water with white wings,
throwing it at the sun, plunging their heads
in and out, and stitching the blue to a lace of foam,

advance in a boisterous phalanx filling their pouches
as they go. When satisfied
with the catch, they wade and waddle into line

upon the shore again to rest, standing or sitting
                as best suits them, leisurely
swallowing the fish in their cheeks. Then they rise
in a flock, circling high in the air, for a long time.

The white pelican builds upon the ground, a nest of sticks
                and twigs upon sage or sedge,
a home with low walls of sand around to guard
the chalk-white eggs, whose surface is rough to the touch
                due to the shell's irregular
thickness. The idea that the pelican feeds its young
from a wound the bird has gashed in its own breast

has no place among the facts, though it endures.

For a Child Frightened by Lightning

First night in our summer house the sky is falling,
breaking away in wide panes that crash in the valley.
And I am watching from an upstairs window,
thinking that thought is next of kin to lightning

when it crosses my mind the boy in bed below
may wake in the arms of terror and a strange house
while I am spellbound by one pine stallion
rearing at a low cloud bridled by lightning.

Then a bedspring creaks and my son runs crying
through darkness streaked and stunned, where I catch him
at the stair in midflight, hold him still running
from the beast that fled the hills to rage inside him.

Now that my child's heart is a study in thunder,
how can I tell him it will not call his name?
Nothing will calm us now short of sunrise,
gathering flowers where the sky has fallen.

Silence

When at last you would not answer me
I listened like a spy at Heaven's door
and conjured up a dawning, soundless country
where thought became its own best orator;

where crickets sang no louder than the moon
and starlight made more music than light rain.
O echo of an echo, reverie,
thunder tiptoed down from the soft mountain

where I filled the air with love words once
and wrote in granite to outlive my age.
Now though I sweep the verses from this page,
the blank space cannot capture that silence.

The New Music

Word-weary, I dream of some Valhalla where
        I hear a god proclaim the swans will sing
once more. I look down from ramparts ranging
        above thunderheads, and glimpse an opal sphere
that glows, and swells until it cracks skywide
        with a silver-winged cyclone of swans who sing
and sing, until the audience of gods there
        staggers like wild ships keeling in a tide.

In sympathy, the humblest of the host
        whispers in my ear: "That world is lost.
The swans have come to return our gift of song.
        Cloud-drifts will unveil a new world soon."
And gazing down again, I see the larks
        from their heaven joyfully descending.

From *The Book of Fortune* (1982)

Climbing

When he gave up mountains he became
a window washer, hoisting himself on block and tackle
fifty stories above the street. For the love of heaven
    is an addiction like stealing
fast time from the round jail of the clock.

He loves high windows. Saves them for last,
looking down on the traffic, crawling workers
whose vision he rinses clean as fresh glass.
Pigeons swing like puppet birds under his hands.
        But does he think downward?

Does he love his fear of the lurking flaw
    in the scaffold, the crack in a faithless plank?
Does he think of the fatal journey
      between his living and his death? No.
He looks in on the nodding accountants, winks

at an astonished secretary who drops her file.
He looks out along miles of reflected rooftops,
        the sky mirrored in the invisible window.
It is like flying on the surface of our lust
        for a visible horizon.

By noon the top windows are clear as a sudden answer,
        at dusk pure gold,
by night they are pure moon blue.
Sadly he rides the elevator down
and starts again at the foot of the blind wall.

The Sentry of Portoferraio

Blame this island town for the broken boy
who keeps his watch high on the falcon fortress.
Blame this town of rose and sea-green stone
stairways, and the daredevil swallows.
Was it not enough that beneath a circus of birds
his eyes should blindly fix upon each other?
Born lame as an old joke
did he have to grow up in such a town
of pinnacles, one cocked leg
cursing the steps that lead him to his home?

Accuse the snake in the cactus, fig, and grape
gathering liquor from the rainless air;
scold fish heads in the monger's stall,
cats on the sill. Charge the parents
of sturdy children whose eyes renew the horizon,
whose legs conquer mountains and pines.
Did we not conspire in narrow prayers,
to divide his share of health among us?
Did we not invest in our cross-eyed sentry
suffering enough to make a nation wise?

It is the fury of providence
to crowd a family of pain into one creature,
then crown him guardian angel of a town.
It is his lonely insistence on Heaven
that leads lovers to the sudden view
of their bodies broken beautifully against themselves,
that leads our village skyward to command
an ocean, rise and stand up to the sun!
But somebody has to pay for the hobbling climb,
somebody has to pay for his double vision.

Portrait of the Photographer

You are in control of the machine.
Driving east from California in three days,
rigged to the steering wheel, accelerator
and brake by pullies,
tendons of wire and stainless steel.
I drag you from the car like a sack of kindling.

Long ago I told the story of your flight
from the window in San Francisco, back
when drugs were cheaper, the living high and fast;
made what myth of it I could in our defense.
Telling the tragedy once is enough, like living it.
Wasted pain to go over it all again.

Eleven years after that fall you come
to see me in this ground-floor lounge
the Church provides us for a studio
because you couldn't make it up my stairs.
I wheel you down the hall, half air, half fire.
No body, but the camera screwed to your chair,

prosthetic, gleaming, formidable,
fashioned for the hand that cannot move
quick as the eye, the starved hand
with no animation nearer than the elbow
to turn the dials and trip the shutter.
No body but the camera! Between us

after fifteen years of love there is
neither distance nor time,
and only flesh enough to make appearances.
Each time I see you seems to be the last,
and so it should always be, with friends.
You tell me you hold on to us like death,

and the camera, commanding "Face the window.
Stretch out on the sofa, hand on your cheek.
Close your eyes. Now open them." So you have
pursued me, shooting away on foot and on wheels
for more than half my life, convinced
there must be something worth preserving.

The room sails into a shadow. You ask me
to look out and give you a reading on the sun.
A low cloud bank, heavy, slowing down.
Gold border turns to purple, then to black.
Not much time. You burrow under the hood.
Focus. My life flickers against the lens.

You slap the negative in, cover the barrel,
then doff the lens cap softly so not to shake
the camera, the furniture, the light.
And maybe this time
if we do not perish first, maybe this second
if we can hold perfectly still

maybe this time, surely by now you have died
enough to take me for what I am
and I can look like the man I have become.

Mannequins

This indecent procession of the undead
invades the Avenue windows, dressed to kill,
sporting tomorrow's clothes and yesterday's faces.

One struts in a velvet shaft of midnight blue,
slashed down the back in a diamond heat of lust,
gold crown at the wrist and throat, a garnet ring.
Here Lucie Anne side-slits a terry dress
trimmed in Venetian lace
and petal edging on the camisole. There a lady
most unladylike, lounges
in silk of liquidly drapable muscadine,
grinning the wine-red of wickedness. Another
borrows the schoolgirl's kiss, the cupie bow,
eyes round and empty as pots, and the apple cheek.
For we also yearn to join the innocent in their clothes:
Jill in her jumper, Johnnie in his jeans,
sheep in their fleece, the pig in his narrow poke.

But I prefer them naked, the posturing frauds,
free from any trace of shame, and without nipples
or the fur that friction-proofs our parts for love.

I like them headless, oh Marie Antoinette,
what beauty knocked in the executioner's bucket!
I like them wigless, as a rack of bullets.
I like when a leg is kicked out of its socket
or an arm flings back in some preposterous gesture
as if to say
"So happy to have missed the agony of meeting you,"
or
"We who are early salute you from the backs of our heads."
I love when the feet swivel for a fast retreat,
and the head jerks in wonder defying the neck.

But when they are assembled and decked out,
they turn vicious, whispering through the glass:
"How have you achieved your shabbiness?
Where is your glamour, the youth you were born with?
Where, if you have one eye, is the other,
and if you have three limbs, where is the fourth?
Where is your hair, marcelled or carefully windblown,
your eyebrows, the artfully painted lips?
Put your face to the glass, you wretched snail,
kiss me, you desecration of a man."

Miami

After years of stock-car racing, running
rifles to Cuba, money from Rio, high
diving from helicopters into the Gulf;
after a life at gunpoint, on a dare,
my father can't make the flight out of Miami.

Turbojets roar and sing, the ground crew
scatters out of the shadow of the plane.
My father undoes his seat belt, makes his way
up the aisle, dead-white and sweating,
ducks out the hatchway, mumbling:
luggage was left at the dock, his watch
in the diner. Head down
he lurches through the accordion boarding tube,
strides the shining wing of the airport, past
windows full of planes and sky, past bars,
candy machines and posters for Broadway shows.
Gasping in the stratosphere of terror, he
bursts through the glass doors and runs
to a little garden near the rental cars.
He sits among the oleanders and palms.

It started with the Bay Bridge.
He couldn't take that steel vault into the blue
above the blue, so much horizon!
Then it was the road itself, the rise and fall,
the continual blind curve.
He hired a chauffeur, he took the train.
Then it was hotels, so many rooms
the same, he had to sleep with the light on.
His courage has shrunk to the size of a window box.

Father who scared the witches and vampires
from my childhood closets, father
who walked before me like a hero's shield

through neighborhoods where hoodlums honed their knives
on concrete, where nerve was law,
who will drive you home from Miami?
You're broke and I'm a thousand miles away
with frightened children of my own.
Who will rescue you from the garden
where jets flash like swords above your head?

Notes for a Conversation with my Grandfather

Nothing but prophecy seems fair,
for the inequity of our separate knowledges
hurts most. I'll come as I am,
a portrait the artist left to chance:
my mouth and hands done justice maybe,
but the eyes and brow a glance and wrinkle shy
of full expression. You are entire,
yet I must face you half made-up,
younger than you were when I was born.

I see you milling in the garden
like St. Francis. Birds and poverty.
I see you stripping the backbone from a fish.
You are floating on a suitcase
in the North Atlantic, riding the whirlpool
over your torpedoed steamer. Shipwrecked
again off the coast of Argentina,
you comb the beach six months,
go begging, carry water for the whores.
You rise from the black ground of photographs,
young rake with derby cocked, propped on a cane,
a plump and laughing girl on your free arm.

Once you drove me through a twilight
landscape December had beaten flat,
to the clearing where a giant holly
fountained berries, held them in spiny leaves
against the sky. A lonely God!
What were you hunting when you found Him there?

Summer, you would gather figs on the bank
of the black and knotted Nanticoke
River you swam at dawn
for twenty years, to keep the body young.
The brown fruit split under your thumb.

Pink meat shone through seed clouds
and clear honey.
                    You lived on air
while holding the fig open for me to enter—

but all this history is out of place.
I meant these words to sound on a live ear.
I'll settle my debts on all experience
in the currency of a plan
or closely figured prophecy.
Maybe we can still meet equally,
as two portraits ruined: yours, a masterpiece
worn by wind and sun;
mine scarred by the painter's rage
for what was promised yet could not be done.

Make my memory as faithful as these plans.
I will be strong. I will be rich
if the world holds,
tell the truth as long as the Truth holds,
love men and women as I have loved you.
Beyond such certainties I will live in the cold
mystery where both of us will die.

Now I am ready to go to you, ready
to pour this wine of our shared harvest . . .
But why am I wavering in the door?
Can I still be wondering if all these words
aren't pilfered? Have I borrowed what is left
of your life and bought another rag
to keep me warm? Why am I shuddering?
Afraid of what the family might think?
What will your daughter, my mother say
if she hears me at your bedside whispering

these love words
as if this were a wedding night?
The boy is selfish, rash and rude
to make this show, this mockery of our grief!
He thinks he's greater than the dying man.

I don't. They never knew my mind.
But someone does. A harsh, all-seeing light
rushes, crowds your room as if the sun
had risen on both sides of us at once.
Daylight without shadow, more terrible than night!
Whatever words I may find fit for me
are too poor to stand in such a light.
I'll keep those promises to myself,
memory, apology, and plan,
not out of some shame or grief,
despair or doubt you would understand.
I'll keep this to myself because it is poor
and nothing short of glory would suffice.

As I enter your room I will be silent
as we imagine the near room to be
awaiting you. Silent
as the crashing wave, the blasted oak
lightning loved and entered
when there were none to witness, none to hear.

Schoolhouses

The staircases are always last to go,
winding into the sky like cries of defiance
against the wrecking ball and dynamite.
And the "up" staircase is still adamantly "up"
though bells are silenced and the rushing students
have all passed on, and "down" is "down" although
there are no more classes above or below.
No matter. Imagination, delighting in space
as does memory, climbs and runs downstairs
stopping to rest at a landing, take in the view
that finally escaped the narrow windows.
It whispers: In this room I learned
numbers refer not to things but to what we think
about things, and down that hall
I fell in love for the first and longest time.
Here I discovered uranium. There, an honest man.
Here I learned the shortest distance between two points
is sleep. There I learned I would die, but not when.

Before the school was leveled it was abandoned
and served as an altar
where the neighborhood children celebrated
their rage against learning. My daughter and I
used to go walking there
to check on the vandals' progress,
windows newly smashed, legends of graffiti,
chairs dismembered, the clock with twisted hands,
books read by rain and fire, their spines crushed.
There is no vandalism so inspired, none so pure
as children's rage against what has loved
and failed them. It is a bitterness of heart.

I want my daughter to see the school
as mortal, nothing like a church.
I came upon one chapel in the woods,

abandoned but intact, the steeple
piercing an overhanging bough,
wrens in the belfry, the rose window
casting its roulette of sunshine
over the scattered pews. And in cities
where the Church has long ceased to serve
the parish they will sometimes comfort the ruin,
board up windows where stained glass was stolen,
consecrate the door with a wreath on Christmas.
Teenagers sneak into the nave, to make love
or drink wine in the enduring sanctuary.
But the school is mortal. Vandals sentence it
and wreckers come to carry out their will.

Now the low cedars press against the wind
in a field that was once schoolyard
and my daughter clings to my hand.
She doesn't know where we are. She
is afraid I am telling the truth:
the school *was* here that now is gone,
and home, bed, mother, father,
are equally frail and liable to disappear.
We circle the site and I am pointing
and explaining—rubble, rubble—
wondering whose locker held the bomb.

How many teachers slept with Valery Strauss?
What are the prime numbers after ninety-seven?
Why is the school more eloquent in this state
than it was in its stern glory when we were young?
And why couldn't the vandals have been entrusted
with the wrecking of the schoolhouse? That
would have been more practical, more humane.
Are they too anarchic to do the job right?
Is it the nature of vandals that

they cannot deliver what they advertise?
The original Vandals were passionate and thorough.
I read about them in Ancient History.
They overran Gaul, Spain, and North Africa,
invaded Italy and sacked Rome destroying
many monuments of art and literature.
The schoolhouse vandals are sneaky, picayune,
anonymous, unworthy of their name.

Why do I take such joy in leading my daughter
on the outskirts of this animated emptiness?
What have I learned in school but the savage joy
of asking questions that brought the building down?
Why have I had to grow old to ask such a question
as why do we have to grow old to become wise?
I suppose I would rather be young and foolish
and probably am, though you'd never know it
to see my grey hair. Joy made me grey.

Lafayette Square

> "The certificate of Coroner Patterson
> in the case of Mrs. Henry Adams, who died suddenly
> in this city on Sunday last, is to the effect that she
> came to her death through an overdose of potassium
> cyanide, administered by herself. She was just
> recovering from a long illness, and had been suffering
> from mental depression. She left no children."
>
> —*The Washington Critic*
> December 9, 1885

Who is it on the stair, who in the hall?
My hemisphere, the master of the house.
More flowers! All the porcelain, love,
is choked with purple iris and carnations—
you garland my room as if I were a corpse.
Did you startle me? Like a baited chain
of mousetraps, my nerves go off at a hair's fall.
You might have tiptoed in on a down cloud
(as you seem to do), your breath hushed,
and still slammed my soul in terror between
the bedroom door and the broken window of my heart,
out of which flies, what? My thought
in letter-winged shape of a white dove.

What was I writing? Oh nothing. What sort
of nothing needs to hide itself from my husband?
Just a note to my sister, news of the day.
"Elms bend with wet snow along a street
mobbed with foreigners rushing on
preposterous errands, Patagonian trade,
treaties, hawking foghorns and elixirs.

The house we are building is almost done.
From my creaking balcony next door
I trap it in my camera: the gargoyle drains,

the corner turret scanning the White House.
Our great lawmakers lodged across the Square
trample on the Mormons and Chinese.
Blaine is called up, Shipherd testifies.
Madame Catalano sails away
to Russia Wednesday next with three
babies, an alligator, a wolfhound.
I have all this by hearsay,
augury and my window's parallax.
For we are declining the circuit of winter teas.
I don't go out. I won't go out at all."

I was about to add:
"Through all the hours of sorrow, my husband
stands like an archangel at my side,
riposting harpies with a paper knife."
Thus I would lie for you, though no one
will ever know the true range of your kindness.
You are the gentle hand holding
the knife to my throat.
Why do you snatch it away?
Now you've scattered the pages on the floor,
go on and read the first lie of the day
in my letter's true address, "Dear Father."

Why do I write to my father, why
should I lie to you, my husband? You shine
your pitiless study lamp into my mind,
plot the navigation of my blood,
tide and wind, my calm and rising gale.
It was only last April that the doctor died
who was my father, and my fever began to rage,
the sickness that is grief unmoved by prayer.
No mother to share my sorrow, none to remember,
no child to nurse and laugh away despair—

Why shouldn't I write to him? The words are mine.
Our Sunday letters held me in his world,
whether I journeyed to hell or Washington.
And who is more distant than the newly dead,
more starved for comfort, love words in the dark?
You, my husband, you, my inquisitor.
Does your jealousy reach into his grave?
I think that he is more alive than you.

And if he's not. Why shouldn't I address the dead?
It is the house profession, the house passion,
your weird Confucian necrology,
stuffing your presidential ancestry
with feathers of shredded fact, excelsior.
My husband is the son of a great house,
the house of Adam, fathers of the tribe
of Adams, unfallen Adams all.
My husband is the end of perfect breeding,
thought out of action, action ended,
the begonia flowering out of a wheatfield.
My husband is the mortician of his clan.
You cram them to the lips and prop them up,
President, Grand-President, Senator,
for all the world as if they were alive.
So they are more alive than you and I
who live across from the ancestral home,
spectral saboteurs of the White House.

Forgive me love. It is the sickness, sickness
of grief and loneliness. He was all
the father and mother I had. Where are my children?
Was there no more room in history
for children? Oh I have heard you mourn
our fated incapacity to bear
another Adam or a dewy Eve,

a child for your knee, another President.
But how does it happen, love, in some
naked space dreamed high above the bed,
or breathing the common air, sharing a thought?
Ideas never made a child, though they kill men.

Forgive me, love, it is the sickness
of December, and loneliness, and irony.
What comfort can you afford, try as you may?
You whisper to my sadness: "All of life
is nothing but a series of farewells.
The bitterest is spoken. Look to the future."
Then you rise, kick open the study door
on such a howling multiverse of dragons
no monk in guilt's traction could conceive:
"A million homicidal engineers
running an ungodly godlike train
a hundred million horsepower full speed
up and down the shrinking landscape.
Space deranged by electricity, horsepower
doubling every fifteen years, the days
of time are numbered in a meteor world
where Rome will no longer be Rome, nor time time.
We are the slaves of coal, die with our master.
Apocalypse by law of logarithms. New York a nest
of twenty million insects in the throes
of metamorphosis, changing worms to wings—"
Enough! Just leave the future to itself!
Must the historian turn to prophecy? Help!
First you drive me into my father's arms,
then you cite your revelation,
that when the body's broken, content spills
into a maze of branching rivulets,
a vapour of quick rainbows in the blue,
a few drops in the reservoir of truth.

Not even my father's ghost can hear me now!
What consolation in your nightmare future
if it is not "Better to be dead?"
Let me follow my father. You live on.

You say I cannot die, "for we are one."
And you have hidden from me, half in jest,
every pointed object in the house,
knives honed for vengeance by the Japanese,
your razor blade, the ivory-handled cutlery.
Your irony is under lock and key
with dueling pistols rusted impotent,
or disguised as an obsequious compassion.
Am I chained to the pleasure of your company?
What am I to you, your wife,
an image at the banquet table's end,
the hostess schooled in fashionable wit,
companion on horseback, partner in despair?
And more than this, when all the guests are gone:
mother, sister, cradle, sepulchre,
repository of such terror and remorse
as only an infant of two hundred years
could know and bawl out in the nursery.
This and more than this. We are not one,
but you have lived within me, crowded
precious space I needed for my soul,
lived within me, not in the happy way
of man in woman, the circle of her arms
to die bodily then rise in love again.
You have fattened in me like
a foetus satisfied to live unborn
in the body of a virgin. I
was the woman you could never be,
nor can I, for the goddess will explode
the strongest temple men can shut her in.

The house we are building is almost done.
From my balcony I've watched it rise
out of the mud, on the backs of laborers
shouldering mortar hods, sinews of brick
to launch in double arches for the portals.
The architect has taught you Romanesque.
Sometimes I think the soul of it is dust
as brick powder sifts into my room
tincturing the windowpane.
Sometimes I think the house is history meant
to be seen from afar, never lived in,
a foursquare, window-slotted monument
three stories high with a turret at the quoin.
I will not live there though it's built for me.
But I have kept a record of the house
in photographs with the tripod camera
you gave me to keep my mind out of the past.
Here is the vacant lot, here is the canyon
delved and blasted out of Lafayette Square.
Here is the first story. Scantlings
of white pine sketch out the halls
of the second story you shall walk alone,
bedroom, dressing room, a suite for guests,
all flooded with skylight, without the walls.
Here you are wrangling with Richardson
whether the parlor window should look out
street-level, or pitch above the roof
of our neighbors across the way,
over the White House toward the whiter sky.
Here is the sea-green, onyx chimney piece.
We wanted purple African porphyry
(a stray vein runs from Braintree to Lynn
under Boston harbor,
diamond-hard, a curse to the quarrymen.)

It was too dear, though nothing be too dear,
and the Mexican onyx glowed so exquisitely
it made your soul yearn, you wrote to me
in the North, while I watched my father die.

So here is the history of our home
from mud to sky,
cobweb of running beams and crossing planks,
the naked corner and the standing wall.
A miracle, this little box, a time machine
where a slide coated in silver collodion
is struck eternal witness to the light.
The camera masters time! In nitrate
solution, silver, and the fixative
potassium cyanide, so deadly some say
three drops in a cup of tea will heat
one's blood to gall and paralyze the heart.

I have planned a portrait of myself
to keep you company when I am indisposed,
so wan and winter-pale
the light cuts through me to the world beyond.
You will forgive me if it is not drawn
as Whistler would have me, or your friend
St. Gaudens might cast his American saint
in the light of science, or as virgin chained
somewhere between the portal and the shrine.
We want something more gothic about the house.
South of the weathervane cocked for a May wind,
north of the red chimney there will break
through solid beam and attic tile and slate,
a slender tower sprung from a broken arch,
unbuttressed, aiming at the infinite.
From the crown of that tower, in full view
of all the capital, I'll wave goodbye . . .

Go on your stroll without me, and forget
all this, forgive my winter weariness,
my anger and my love if it proves cruel.
Solstice cautions the daylight and I weep
for the absence winter glorifies to a season,
glazing nature, widowing the world.
Leave me to my work, my solitude.
The picture will be waiting when you return.

Letter to Thomas Edison from John Burroughs

To Thomas Edison, Menlo Park, New Jersey

April 21, 1916

Dear Thomas,
As you brought light into the world
let me call the sound of April into your silence,
for April is in heat and pairing with the sun
in my vineyard.
Meadowlark on the hickory, his high note flies
like the shaft from a crossbow.
Bobolink's in the hill meadow singing of boyhood.
Surely birds were hatched in a human heart
for the bluebird warbles of home, the catbird pride,
and my red-eyed vireo preaches peace of mind.
Oh the triumph of a robin, faith of the sparrow!
A sheaf of reedy willow-brook notes
the red-winged blackbirds play
in orchards piled to the clouds with apple-bloom.
Under-hill the highhole calls, voice from the soul
of April, the new furrow, seed and the planting.
Bees hum, the air is strung with a resonant chord.

Highhole calls again from the currant patch:
Go and spade horseradish, spinach
and melting roots of parsnip. Let us taste the soil!
Earth is ripe for the plough, it lusts for it.
I mark out the grape trenches, open furrows
for young vines. I guide the team of horses.

Make room for my vineyard, dig out place-rock
where it peeks from the turf.
We break the stoney sleep of ages
with bars and wedges probing, with dynamite blasting.
Where no sun has shone in a million years

we let it in,
and sometimes we find green lichen in buried stone.
O life will work in the merest crack or chink!
Twilight, and I am glowing head to foot,
fresh from the earth-bath.
In every cell of my brain I feel the land
newly plowed. The furrow has struck in
and sunlight has photographed it on my soul.

Now my landscape floats into the sky, my cup
brims, the horizon swims with divine elixir.
The walls of my self are glass. I see through pores of my skin.
Laws of nature joining the part to the whole,
the holy nerves of the universe are laid open
like a spider web glossed with dew and morning light.
My thoughts go scratch with hens in the dry leaves,
with geese nipping spears of grass.
My thoughts fly north with ducks migrating,
hover about the farm and garden fires.
They career away to the sugar maple woods
where sap is clinking slowly in tin buckets.
Man is a pace of earth and a rag of sky
and laws of the outer world are born in him.

Forgive me, friend, I wander from pure music
to pure thought, where I have no license,
and such thoughts need no cracked horn to trumpet them.
They are the inward coda of our age.
I had to live seventy years to see such a Spring!
To see it, Thomas, not that it wasn't there
inside me, the calendar furled in a catkin.

Which leads to my greater purpose. Could there be
something greater than playing Nature's phonograph
for the Wizard of Menlo Park, the music lover

who can't hear the robin's racket, the blackbirds jangling?
Yes! For you read my letters and books, you
who do not need them, whose soul is so high-domed
it spans my hillocks, and the mountains and seas.
Adam never walked in so rich a garden.
It is not for you, but for our mutual friend
I mimic the meadowlark and the highhole.
I write you what I fear he'll never read
because he is restless, worse than deaf and blind.
I write you what Henry Ford will not hear from me.

Remember our last excursion, the caravan
                    of millionaires gone vagabond under my wing,
Ford, Firestone, and I, your faithful guide,
                    naming birds and leaves, reading the stars,
leading our motorcade through the Adirondacks.
Somewhere near Vermont a car broke down.
When the village mechanic blamed the motor,
Henry coughed and tipped his battered derby.
"I am Henry Ford," he said. "I say
this motor is running perfectly." The rustic paled.
He said, "Well, then the electric spark has failed."
"I am Thomas Edison," you growled.
"I say there is nothing wrong with the wiring."
The mechanic looked to heaven, then to me,
my laughing, wrinkled cheeks, my beard of snow,
and said "I suppose this must be Santa Claus!"

And so I do remain to Henry Ford:
Saint John, kind John, bird man of the Catskills,
fit to name the beasts as Adam, and as innocent.
"Bring John along and leave the books at home,"
he says and then kidnaps me from the farm.
Don't get me wrong. You know I love the man,
    the fire of his will, his diamond pride.

But I fear for him as I would for my own son
if he seemed so ill-equipped to die.
You might say it were well enough to be equipped
        to live, at Ford's age. So would I
if it were enough for the man to live for himself.
But you who shed your light upon so many,
        know the inventor lives not for himself
but for the inheritors of what he finds.
Such living wants a sense of death as well,
        and Henry doesn't see that he will die.

Tell us the symptoms of his malady,
        case history and prognosis, Dr. Burroughs!
A farmboy in love with birds and plough horses
            gets lost in a busted watch and wanders
for days among twirling gears and spiral springs.
By the time he finds his way back to the world
                    the lark has grown a pulsating halo
of functional definition, the lark lives
                        to keep the greedy locust from the corn.
Rivers that once ran only to dazzle him
                            now bend to nurse the pasture,
seeds are to split, and sprouts to branch and blossom,
flowers to lure the bee making liquor of light.
The waterpump is seven times more beautiful
                    than idle rainbows haunting the fans of spray.
Handle finds its door, lock finds its key,
                        sunup, sundown, moon and tide and wind
likewise learn their places and their uses.
Father, mother, autumn, clock and chime
                            forge their ineluctable chains of music,
rapid and passionate as the boy's heart.
On his mother's death he writes this elegy:
"The house is like a watch missing its mainspring."
Here's less than Truth and more than Poetry!

Henry sees himself as a cocked piston,
          discrete, at the heart of a fabulous machine
that might run smoothly through the universe
               making us kind and clean and prosperous
if only the parts would let him assemble them.

He moved from watch to clock, from the clock case
to the booming chambers of a steam engine,
from steam to gas that fueled his motorcar,
from car to factory. There every man
played his part, turning creation into fate,
an empire of spidery banging Model-T's
cast in Ford's image, burning the roads of America.

Where did we last see him? On the deck
of the S.S. *Oscar,* the "Peace Ship" bound for Norway
that Henry chartered out of pocket
"to bring the boys home from the trenches by Christmas."
Wilson couldn't, nor could Sir Edward Grey,
but Ford with his cargo of crackpots and one idea
would stop it. "Money lenders made the war.
Sell tractors instead of guns and they'll come home."
A band played drums and brasses above the crowd
that waved handkerchiefs and wept and cheered.
Some leapt into the water, and some sang,
and Ford, throwing roses from the rail,
offered you a "million" if you'd go. You didn't hear.

He's home now, blaming the newspapers and Jews.
War goes on, the Kaiser wants the sea and land.
Henry wants to run for President.
President! He cannot name five Presidents!
The father of so much power in the world,
looks on history like his bastard son,
a shabby accident, an old disgrace,

the best-forgotten folly of his youth.
His present eclipses all our past. Yet
what is power? Did you think Niagara Falls
crashing through daylight, a great display?
What lies silent in the earth around,
of which Niagara only whispers a phrase?
Power is gravity claiming its own,
the lust of rain to blend with sea again.
Man sets his oaken wheel between two waves
and gravity mulls his wheat. All life
and movement is in breaking the equilibrium.
But, from drop to wave to paddle wheel and mill,
all things are an arch and every rising stone
is a keystone. You cannot move a single rock
without the risk of bringing the building down.

Talk to him, Thomas. He'll listen to you.
I show him a waterfall and he builds a plant.
I show him the birds of the Everglades
and he returns from Europe with a shrieking cage
of songbirds to set loose in America:
rare parakeets and Moorish nightingales,
birds that scarce could live where they were born.
Tell the man his head is full of birds,
his heart a spring chorus if he would listen!
You are his hero, his idol, the only one
in whom he sees himself as more himself
than he is, one in whom he sees
his own green thoughts and instincts ripened,
full grapes on your vine, rounded in sunlight.
He sees you in himself. I hope he's right.

When I think how different my light could have been,
your light, that warms my page after sundown
    and makes the night my study!

I wonder if the bulb you made would shine
the same if you had been a different man.
Would it sweep the shadows from the rafter cracks
and corners if you had not known
some child might need the comfort of light there?
Would it spark the wrinkles of my brain
with morning wakefulness had you not known
daylight never sleeps in the human mind?
Suppose you had been a bitter, sullen man,
a hermit or churl. You might have made
light that rides only the surface of things,
fit to find our way from room to room
but not to trace the corridors of thought
where humor slaps its thigh or revery sees
tide rip the winter waves to ragged foam.
You saw how daylight bronzes naked skin, then shines
right through the skull to blood and bones and heart.
You took no model but the sun, made light
to heal and pray by, light to make love by.
Mimic only the sun, my children. And like him
grow larger at thy setting!
Man's triumph comes in the way of Nature's will.
She calls to him:
"My horses are flying this way, vault into the saddle
and ride along or be trampled if you fall.
My steam will ferry you and your household
around the globe if you can harness it,
or rend you to atoms if you miss your hold.
My streams will saw your lumber, grind your wheat
or grind you if you lose the upper hand."
Man appeared and man will disappear, time
squanders him recklessly as autumn leaves.
What could nature care when it is her own
coffers death enriches, what can she care
if we are all blown back to the sun and stars?

Think of all Ford has done, what he might do,
and you and I in our graves.
He made a motorcar. Well enough!
It is a blind and desperate thing
ready to roll in a ditch or climb a tree.
Could he have built the machine with more sympathy?
Yesterday I came from driving my son to the station.
I aimed my new Ford at the old barn
door. Then I got rattled, the car ran wild,
burst through barnside with a splintering crash
of boards and timbers, cats and chickens crazed.
Rolling to the cliff's edge, the flywheel caught
on a rock that took more pity on me
or I would have landed on the other side of Jordan.
Thus fear delivers us to the thing we fear.
I knew it would happen. Talk to him, Thomas.
He may make a machine
to transport us from New York to Baltimore
or this world to the next by distillation
of bodies into the soul's electric charge.
All well enough! Bravo! First make him see
the universe that is one human soul
lest the future traveller
arrive without his proper past, his father's wish,
the rainbow's logic, and his mother's pride.

Jubilee of goldfinches in the elms. They come
every spring to these trees on the same day
as if by harmony of common mind.
They invade the vineyards and the garden
for green seeds of chickweed,
they attack the shut dandelions,
they feed on hatching elmseeds
rifling the winged disk of its germ.

No bird has so pretty a way of match-making, they join
in singing each other's praises.
What is their song? Of luminous greenness everywhere
as leaves let the light shine through.
For nature is young, we can see the blood in her veins,
her skin is so delicate and thin.
Morning is a pale youth, a nude maiden
veiled by her own hair.
O the shy blossom of hazel and butternut
and the river shimmering through green mist!
New time always, the verge of time, the days turning
their beautiful sad faces toward us.
The days are children. We have them a little while
and then they are taken from us.
Mossy boulder, milk of the black birch,
scent of meadow rue and ginger-root
with dusky floral bell, white trillium.
If fortune filled only the measure of man's dream
we should all be buried in debt.
If I think my will is free, that's good enough!

Skylark climbs in a spiral wing-song, trailing
sparks of melody, crowns his flight
with ecstatic trills against the brilliant sky.
The best time is coming, time to make sacred in passing,
time of the greatest milk yield, succulent grass,
clover fresh in the fields and sweet syringa
about the house, and daisies and buttercups.
Scent of blooming rye fields and wild grape
and the calmer song of birds, their first madness
and lovemaking over.

Come Thomas, leave your shop while we have time
and let's take to the open road for the strawberry days!

Ode to Virgil

1

Astral mechanic! Forecaster of empires! Vergilius!
The children of Europe are gathering under your stars.
They throng the dialectical Squares and Roundabouts.
They are marching through medieval walls and streets
under flags all the colors of your far-flung planets.
The children of Europe are marching into the constellation
  of Orion
under the blue flag of morning, marching under red flags
into their parents' bedrooms at the instant of conception,
marching under black flags into the death camps!
They are cracking the armored seed of history, storming
your citadels in divine frenzy, like locomotive sunflowers.

Children of Berlin drive the Mercedes through a wall
of political graffiti, swastikas, hammers, multi-lingual
  sexual puns,
the blue children of Prague weep into the crockery.
The children of Paris cry all the way to the altar,
children of Belgrade ball into the mouths of cannon,
the children of Berlin cry all the way to the bank.
They are mourning the death of Marx who died
from turning over too many times in his grave.
Red flags at half-mast flutter on the slack lanyards.

They are mourning the deaths of Locke and Rousseau
who died of cancer, flaking away in golden parchments.
Their blue flags mirror stars half-mast in heaven,
white flags flame to black tatters.

The children of Europe are striking, Virgil
and Rome is paralyzed. Nothing works.
The docks are striking, and airplanes and freight-trains,
gears are locked, the dynamos freeze, the piston sticks.

The gas and electric are striking
and the mail and the refrigerators and televisions.
The Gypsies are striking in the Piazza Navona,
their children have been starving for centuries;
the whores are striking on the Via Veneto,
everybody is lying down on the job.
There is a general strike and there are all the little strikes.
I myself am striking in self-defense.
Vergilius Maro, this is your American correspondent in Rome,
Dateline Friday, April 14, 1978, submitted not only with
due respect, but the utmost admiration.

2

Praise Vergilius, patron saint of Ford and Edison,
for he built a bridge of air that would take him anywhere
and spun from silver a mirror that could see
a distance of seven days journey, intrigues and traitors.
Good work Vergilius! The art of sorcery is in a sorry decline!
What sports car will hold the roads
that tunnel our psychic ocean, span the mountains of the sky?
What T.V. news broadcast can bring us tomorrow?

Praise Vergilius the seismograph, his brass archer
stood in the herb garden at Monte Vergine
with drawn bow threatening Vesuvius;
praise the prophylactic insecticide, the brazen fly
by mathematical art disposed in a gateway,
which kept a plague of flies from the city of Naples!
Praise the father of Frigidaire and packaged foods,
whose market kept meat fresh 500 years.

Praise Vergilius, rake and cocksman
for he fell in love with Nero's daughter
who invited him up to her tower in a basket

at midnight, then left him dangling in midair
for all the folks of Rome to see at dawn.
Praise Vergilius, master of revenge, for in his rage
he put out the fires of Rome
and made the citizens kindle their torches one by one
on her nude body bent over in the Forum.

Praise Vergilius, father of public works and central intelligence,
for he devised the Salvatio Romae, palace of bronze
to house a delegation of graven heralds.
When a province revolted its mannequin rang a bell,
the bronze horseman atop the palace shook his spear
and aimed it at the province in revolt.
Praise Vergilius the prophet who claimed his security system
would last until a virgin should bear a child.

3

Pneumatic sage, son of the Empire, come home!
Your villa is on fire! Vergilius, all is forgiven!
St. Paul regrets you died too soon to be converted.
He was looking for you all over the Compagna.
Deep underground your specter sat at a table
piled high with books, meditating under two candles.
Our lean Saint entered the cave mouth, when:
thunderclap, copper archers shot out the lights
and sage and study fell to ashes.

Vergilius, your children are burning, crossing the streets
under red flags against red lights.
They love red the color of rage and fire and blood,
as they love the crucifixion and ritual murder.
They love red the apple and red the devil and red the dress,
red the mouth and red the threshold of twilight.
Traffic snarls in the Piazza Venezia. Down with Mussolini!

they cry, fifty years too late. Machine guns
bristle around parliament because your children
have taken to kidnapping the ancient senators.
They are following your stars, Vergilius,
because that's the way you left them.

Snow in Madrid, Franco haunts the bullring
like a castrated matador.
Fog in Paris, de Gaulle's tenacious ghost
is kicking calcified shit in the Bastille.
Is this your terrible beauty, Father William?
A plastic restoration of Cologne as real as life
with a scarred Cathedral for reproach?
Churches survive but what god will survive the churches?
How can a poor traveller think with all this racket?

Hush children, America is sleeping, her sun
lags half a day behind. Sweet dreams, America!
Hush children and hear the story of an orphan
adopted, buried, and raised by the kind magician.

From *Young Men's Gold* (1978)

for Linda Stevens

In a Free Country

In a free country I would be shot for my thoughts of you.
Where thought was free as radio waves
    my mind would broadcast your outrageous beauty.
Naked phantoms of our wild nights
    would take every mind by storm.
In your name the slaves of industry and commerce
  would revolt, cops would strike,
truck drivers walk off whistling from their loads.
All creatures of the earth would drop their pants
  in tribute, they would fornicate pell-mell,
every man, queen, woman, dyke, and child.
The old would have the young, every mother her son.
And I would be hunted down, my brain quarantined
    in a free country, thinking these last thoughts of you.

How to Survive Heaven

I was touching her where she'd never been touched.
The devil was in me. I said:
"If there is no more to heaven than this
    I am as good as a dead man."
And she said: "What did you have in mind?"

So I opened one door on a white blizzard of stars,
and one to an avalanche of green that was our spring.
When I opened a third we lost our solitude
        to a grey parade of souls come down on a rainbow.
"You think big," she said, "beyond immortality and bliss."

Then this lady, with a wisdom beyond her years,
(I'm sure that she has been to heaven before
        and knows the ins and outs)
gave me fair warning:
"Lie to the angels about your dreams

            or they will confiscate them at the gates
and banish them to the bedrooms of the world.
If there are ghosts around us love,
                they are dead men's dreams
no saint could smuggle into paradise."

"La Belle Dame Sans Merci"

By the road I saw a sleeping woman
more beautiful than the hovering dream
that battled a nightmare above her head.

And in the forest clearing of her dream
stood a hive of worlds, a honeycomb
where destiny had eaten passageways.
Every cell contained a kingdom and a king
named for his ruling passion and his laws.

I am a cruel judge of nature's kindnesses.
And yet I listened
while each one sang out the ballad of his name,
the voices mellow as a bee's last hoard.
Each king sang in his turn

of Compassion, Grace, Love, Charity, and Joy.
Then Beauty rose
and a hawk dived with a nightmare in his claws.

Let sleeping beauty lie, I thought.
The lashes of her eyes were skirts that fluttered
as the long horses of her dreams raced under them,
her hair a swirl of midnight at high noon.
And as I brushed the nightmare from her brow

she woke and began to glow
like a pale bird glutted with fireflies.
She sat and sang to me
with such sweetness of calm hatred and revenge
I hear her song alone.

The Late Visitor

A lady comes to me at an ungodly hour
          and takes off her clothes,
she takes off my clothes. She sits
impossibly calm in the pouring light
of a lamp outside my window.

She reminds me we were immortal,
sloughing our worn skins
every spring, until
one beautiful woman kept her flesh
for fear a lover would not know her.

My lady casts no shadow.
She is clear glass
for inquisitive spirits.
The mirrors in my house
will have nothing to do with her.

Night Medallion

My woman is sharper than new truth,
          a clean bullet hole in thick glass.
Winter cuts its teeth on her, the sun
                cuts its hand on her,
she's too hot for the beach, the golden sand
    goes all to white crystal under her.

She's so proud, the full moon is her mirror.
When she turns from me I see her face
                              in the rolling window of heaven
and when she comes barefoot to my bedside,
               holding a candle,
an elf skates on my heartstream.
Eager candle, milk my mind of treasons.
She's young and I want to fill her with the world.

After the Wedding Party

A white-faced mummer bride
                    and bridegroom antic for the crowd.
They hope the mock veil and stovepipe hat
      will decoy what spirits plot
love's ruin: dead fathers, by-gone lovers,
           imps of cross-purpose
that twist the sheets and spoil a mother's milk.

And so God speeds the true newlyweds
                    in immaculate wishes of good will.
Hell's guard is down, they steal away
like the sly heroes at the crossroads in old westerns
      who get down and walk
while villains chase their riderless horses.

But the lovers have more than clowns and God
            to thank for their freedom.
The groom's mother
                     has taken the devils on herself.
They flutter in her lace bodice
        like young crows.

Poverty

You call to me as if I were in some other bed
  or gone gold digging with the sun. In fact
I was dreaming I had ten minutes to haul a fortune
  in jewels and coins from the cache of a secret mountain.
An underground river bolted under my boat,
  spilled the loot and rushed me back here penniless.
All I could bring home you're holding now
  in your hands, the rippling wings of my proud rising.

Tired of small secrets, little gifts,
  I conjure this secret mountain between us.
Behold the range of my discretion, even in dreams
    when you challenge me from every wind of the compass!
You call to me as from a tall house gratefully burning
   while fortunes panic around us, fall like stars.

The Dance

Fast clouds, in a big hurry to rain on somebody
        but there's blue sky enough for us.
October trees, out of their minds with color,
and you and me like nothing else alive,
        cosmic accidents spawned between better judgments.
How can we bring a child into the world?
Everywhere people are starving, loveless, climbing walls,
and here we're hugging and kissing in front of God and everybody
in a park full of cheering trees
and our baby is doing a popular dance in your belly.
There isn't room in our bodies for all this joy!

The Catch

Under the dome of hemlocks
a green pool
where the creek breaks
its fall, a boy kneeled
fishing. You were afraid
our baby might spoil
his catch with her singing.
Then you were amazed
at his concentration
on the red bobber
and the sly shadows
that streak like trout,
the fast wishes
a boy mistakes
for the game of his mind.

I'm not superstitious
but I wondered if
the violet butterfly
haunting us in circles
was the soul
of that child's curiosity,
too polite and shy to make
eyes at you openly.
When you lifted your blouse
to feed our daughter
I know he saw that,
the round white gift
he is too old to cry,
too young to sing for.

He reeled his line,
took off for higher ground.

When I looked again
there was a man
his father's age
who smiled at us unabashed.

On a Winter Morning

Running for the bus
I ripped my hand open
on a parking sign.
I was bringing you roses.
They were shivering
in green tissue
in my left hand
when my right caught
the blade of a misdemeanor.
My knuckle bone smiled
like a beaten fighter
then the blood came in bracelets.

I treasured them in the tissue,
swung aboard, paid my fare
and passed into the aisle
of faces shining
on my new hand.
Old men and young girls
stood up for me, offered
their old and new blood,
the family jewels
of America, priding themselves
on my deep color.

Their eyes said take
what you need to see
from us, their arms said
take what you need to walk,
their lips said our bodies
are full of what you wear
on your white sleeve.

Pro Patria Mori

Our city has never been bombed from the air—
long live our city! Sly providential fathers
        always ship the war into enemy territory,
Tripoli, Nagasaki, the Balkans, Berlin,
their battlefields, their soldiers, their porcelain cities.
But we have our civic monuments to pain.

On my street a roofless mystery of brick
        looks from a shot-through tower over the town.
Old brick, you climbed the air on the shoulders of giants
and will survive my bewilderment, holding your own
against the damnation of rain, adverse starlight
        and curses of enemies weary from oceans of travel,
enemies long dead or aged to lean demons of rancor.
If ghosts had the power of death they were born with
        there'd be more ruin here and less mystery.

I like to know my neighbors. So
I introduced myself in the wild yard
whose bushes have made a pact against invaders,
        and waited to hear the ruin tell me its name
and origins, but got no comment. Just an ad
        painted in slick billboard style of the twenties:
"Cloud Mattresses, the sleep that is forever,"
          and a fading girl
dreaming in the sky against the wall.

Nobody knew it for anything but a ruin.
You'd think the builder had nothing more in mind
than a refuge for lost thoughts, or a rich joke
    on passers-by with nothing better to do
than ponder the reasons for unreasonable things.

        There is a guardian Saint of idlers
who loves me like a son. He must have sent the ghost

who climbed my curiosity with me
into that penitentiary of galleried stillness.
His voice was as soft as my own thoughts:

"They are all gone, the women who manned the machines,
asleep in the sky or riding some senescent island
of guiltlessness. When they were young
they made death for a living.
They left the world behind, like a column of nuns
habited spare of trinkets and silken dainty
underthings that might kiss a spark between their legs
and blow them all into heaven.
The roof was thin sheet metal, to that purpose,
the walls of their cubicles earth-worked iron-strong,
jaws of a monster cannon
to shoot them up and out, so one girl's mistake
wouldn't blow the whole bomb factory like a bomb.

"On this floor they worked in threes like the fates.
One girl fills a brass cup with the powder,
one weighs the charge and hands it on to a third
who stitches the muffin bag for howitzer cannon.
Now, on to the second story—the powder rooms, the vats
from which death drifted in seas, dropped in dumbwaiters.
Black haze. A girl who wore her vanity for a cap
struck a match for her cigarette on the way home
and her dusty coiffure went off like a flashbulb.

"The top story, that now opens on the sky,
is still guarded by a locked brass door.
High level security. Old men outnumbered the women
there, and the workers were larger than their machines.

"How they must have believed in us, as they came to work
in the mouth of this loaded cannon! Their precious work,

the words and ideas, the explaining
    to generals, politicians, bombardiers,
to themselves and maybe to God, at that high level.

"Who ever saw so many lightning rods
on a Christian building? One divine tantrum
might have blown us all into the arms of our enemies.
Now go home, my son. There's nothing more
to see or say, and your time is running out."

No, wait. What's above us? But now he's gone.
The sky is clear and blue through the air shaft,
    through the stair windows, blue as the eyes of angels,
young angels, born young who died young and haunt good weather.

I don't believe the emptiness, my astonishment
keeps climbing the concrete stairs into lying silence,
    sins of omission and abandonment,
looking for women working the death machines
or men thinking above them, men dying below.
Their nightmare pageantry is wasted on me.
I can't believe a word of it, a book,
a countryside of graves thrown from these ruins
or the dragon teeth of their broken, mythic stones.

Old Man at the Wood's Edge

Leaves, dry skirt of the wind, lie down by me
        and don't blow away.
Sky is low, the sun's in hiding,
    this masterless winter like a cataract
of broken days, has made
        a tombstone quarry of these hills.
The woods are full of skeletons and the closets
are full of orphaned saplings, birds
nursed in their chilled arms, perched
    on their white shoulders.

I made this cold in the raw image of my absence
so that I might know revenge for my own death.
It is a violent, senseless act, like all acts of love.
I hang the moon in my heart,
        sweep the sky of stars.
My children must learn to find their way in the dark.
I am a hard river, a misfortune
        without pity. When I go down
I'm taking the summer with me.

Old Man by the River

Flood tide, boats glide high above the bank,
gay lilies crane to look into the sun.
What kind of friends would leave me here alone,
an empty house behind me, a full graveyard
ranging from my door to the garrulous river?
Kind friends, and true, to leave me with my thoughts.
My teeth are gone, my hair's a white cyclone;
I have more secrets than heaven will ever know.
Take my daffodils, what a bargain of light
for the reckless April that discovers them!
Little girls with lightning-quick hands
arrest the leaping blossoms in midflight
and lay them on my doorstep in the night.
Today I scared the boy who brings the news.
I am a weathered man the adventure of whose
    conversation nature has immured.
Three walls are deadpan stone, the last is the river.
Who will I talk to when the river runs away?

Rip Van Winkle

Whose hands are these, whose blanket of whiskers?

I must have fallen a long way in my sleep
to land in this circle of wild phlox.
Last I remember it was autumn
and I was in a young man's rage
over some woman, I have forgotten,
who sent a floating puppet of herself
to tell me she would never come again.
When she had gone, I lay down in this grove
and sleep came over me like a gentling music.

Now I've slept the heart of my life away
and nothing to show for it but this dream:
I swore I'd take these faithless woods alive
  to burn like a candle in the attic
of my remorse. And all I vowed was by my will
as good as done. I climbed the fire tower
and saw it all go to hell,
leaf by leaf, mountain by mountain, storm by storm,
every elm bark and wind that knew her name.

It's better for the birds I slept so long.
Sure as hell I would have burned this forest down
    and lived to be more lonely than I am.

Better to wake on the right side of one's life
in a clear season, and see the forest for the trees,
   each one in complete possession of itself.
The years I lost are winter to this spring.
It's good green, and a kind shade for my old head.

Echo

The wind that leaves the fisherman in peace
assaults the blue hills, the wooded mountain
like a caravan of gypsies in old Fords
abandoning Illinois
to plunder the rural groceries of New England.

So the man at sea-level can look the sea in the eye
and know his own power, vis-a-vis
tame breakers making their mark against his shore.
Whereas the high numbers of the upland storm
howl through the breathless zero of one's will.

Right now a tree is falling and nobody to catch it
but a sleeping tramp, a maverick gypsy cipher
who's forgotten who and where he is,
his mother and child, the birdsong and mayapple,
the sun on his cheeks and the path he took to bed.

Summer House

1

Miles from town the long arm of the world
pursues me in the disguise of rivers and meadows,
a cheap trick she plays but I have to laugh
        and go along for the ride.
Same light and wind and wind and light,
            heroes who make the history of the day.
Clouds exiled from northern storms
                glide out from the nape of a mountain,
white targets on a shooting gallery range.
Ladders of getaway light drop from the clouds.

2

Old eagle mounts cross-drafts over the pines,
        circling for slow rabbits,
young hawk scouts a ravine for challenges.
Sheep strum a field of walking daisies,
        pluck spikelets of couch grass;
day lilies chafe high collars of dagger fronds.
Mad architect pitched my roof at the world's end
and like Noah I want to bring everything into the house,
        at least a photo and a name for each,
light for my walls and a spell against silence.

3

But something resists, Great Nature or my little one
like a rich man's mistress embarrassed suddenly
by her position in the scheme of his affections.
When power drives the body to acts of love,
        love takes the first flight out.
And the best company, like the worst, arrives uninvited.
There is the heart's desire for a full house and then

there is the danger of friends as the leaves of the forest
veiling the dance of naked trees,
the skeleton with whom you must at last lie down.

4

When mind is coterminal with nature's body
they hum like spent lovers in a bed of silence, rich
    as suspended applause, or counsel
so wise and potent we reserve it for ourselves.
Such full loneliness presages cordial death.
But this house reminds me I am far from home.
Men in strict training for a meaner death
keep to themselves like this
in solemn imitation of their enemy, hoping
he'll think they're part of him and pass on.

5

I would be a better neighbor to the unknown
if I could round up the vagabonds of my world
and take them on the road with me when I go
to some ghost town that has forgotten
the jugglers of the wind, the high-handed clown
of sunshine, the stallion of love that leaps the hoop
flaming eternally between my life and death.
Surely we're allowed to take what we can carry
and maybe my show would bring children to the streets
and women to the windows of that sleeping town.

6

Night has slipped under the blanket of the lake.
Tideless waves throw wings of light on the sandy floor,
    nerve on nerve of gold underwater birds.

Earth's historians, wind and light protect their sources.
But I'll bet wind comes from the spaces dead men leave
        and raw light rises from tombs.
Too gothic perhaps, but I swear
there is no greater truth in the storm and sun
whose riddles surround us like the horizon
no man can see without turning his back on it.

Sunday

When the bat got in before dawn
he brought the darkest of the night with him.
Wings beat whispers above our bed
          and a vigilant instinct woke us shuddering.
Radar told us something was flying around
up there and it was no nightmare
but the very form of fear, its content unknown,
a shadow strayed from the cave and the church tower.
I opened the window but he stayed with us
      circling the room like a black halo
until daybreak when he could glide out on the wings
          of our vision, a brighter way of flying.

From *The Follies* (1977)

The Follies

Blind Mr. Klugel loves the baritone of Mr. Cantini.

Mr. Klugel rocks on the back porch, listening
while his wife begins her nightly striptease
          in the bright showcase of her bedroom window:
a benefit for the ragged voyeurs of the South City
     who can look but cannot touch.

Time for all good children to be in bed.

From the tar roof of a row house over the wharves
     pours the wide baritone of the moderately drunk Mr. Cantini
singing the sun into a new country, singing
the boats to sleep in their slips, taming the oil rainbows
          to a flat shimmer in the harbor lights,
calling the stevedores to battle in dockside bars and blank alleys,
tuning up the full moon chorus of neighborhood dogs,
          summoning the sluggard moon,
waking up everybody's children.

Dutch

Dutch in the wire cage, burning away with electrified stylus,
        or working the dye in slow along the pinpricks,
a handful of flesh at a time. High musk
of burnt flesh like the backstreet meat markets.
            He is some kind of artist.

My mother thought otherwise, jerking coke at the bar,
            six months out of the flatlands
she married into this garden of earthly delights:
        the ninth street shooting gallery, peep show carnival
and Dutch the tattooist,
a living advertisement of his own genius
                                    and the skill of his masters,
not a square foot of unadorned flesh on his whole body.

She would lead the drunk boys out by the elbow,
            whispering "this is no way to prove yourself a man,"
recalling her uncle Mack raving drunk
            clawing at vein-blue snakes drawn up his arms,
or a tale her sailor father told
                  of a Swedish boy shy of the needle,
who dreamed his fear out loud
                  and woke tangled in the ship's hammock,
twisted in a nightmare and the crew knew it.

And how they pitched in to get the young Swede drunk
              and strapped him to the mess table
and hired a French tattooist
aboard with his packet of needles and rare dyes.
He worked a great clipper ship on the boy's chest
              with square rigging
where wind would catch full in the sails when the blood cleared.

My mother would lead them away from the wire cage
while her father-in-law shouted to his son from the cash register:
        "You bring a *shiksa* into a place of business . . ."
and mother:
                "What kind of a Jew grows rich
                                from writing on a man's body?
            Your laws cry out against it."
And the old man again:
"We are not Gods to make our laws for other men."

I write on your clean skin, my people,
        and then dream the world will see you as you were made.

Cash Only, No Refund, No Return

Earl stood on two legs when he had one to spare,
    then on one leg when the cancer got him,
a short leg and a wicked crutch.
By his own count Earl was accomplice to thirty-four
    murders, ninety-two muggings, and five suicides.
His finger followed the headlines in the paper
    spread out on a glass case that bristled with knives:
Florentine daggers, Arkansas toothpicks,
black bone and pearl-handled stilettos with blades
that kick loose and lock fast with a flick of the wrist,
Turkish daggers with serpentine blades
        to snake the guts from the meanest vendetta.

He stood there in the back end of the arcade
        and they came to him
from bars, the precinct lock-up, from flophouses,
whore houses, foreclosed houses, faithless wives,
good friends gone bad, betrayals, threats, divorces.
Earl had the voice and nose of Jimmie Durante
        and knew how to sell knives.
He just stood there behind the display case.

The Man without Legs

The man without legs has huge arms.
He rolls himself along Park Avenue on a skateboard,
    pawing the concrete with rubber knuckles.
Sparks fly from the steel wheels of his skates.
The man without legs is the quietest beggar in the city
and makes $225.00 a week after expenses.
He looks straight ahead.
He knows pity from the inside out.

At the Millinery Shop

She wants what no clerk in the city can bring her,
        a hat that will make up her mind.
White satin speaks to the red in her cheeks,
                red satin to the white.
Blue crepe shades the clear well of her eye.

She wants a hat to fit her head like an idea
        so perfect only she could have dreamed it up,
a hat that draws attention to itself by disappearing
                and to the head by building on it
a profusion of silent worlds in incomparable colors.

She wants a hat that can think for itself,
                    that will select the proper head for its household.
She turns her back on the round table-mirror
    and a garden of hats on spindles,
admiring the beige lid with a feathery band.

Holding it at arm's length,
                                her eyes half-closed,
she leans back
under a straw bonnet crowned with flowers
          that casually tries itself on her.

Mademoiselle Malo

Pointed ears emerge but head first
            from the voluminous cloak of Mademoiselle Malo.
Her small hands lie in the black lap folds
   like sleeping quail. Butter would not melt
in her mouth, but she should know better
            than to allow her thoughts to run so far, unchaperoned,
from the lighthouse of her mind.

Chrysanthemums flock to the space around her head
   on holiday, and in her head for all we know.
No comment, says the placard on the door
            of her face, no comment.
And that's how a rumor starts, mystery tunneling

like willow roots, greater than trees.
She has turned her best face from us
            and is long gone, her laughing mouth,
eyes of the stormless Atlantic under one star,
   in silent discourse with an inward companion,
some prodigy of love, a small portable god.

The flowers clamor for attention, plead and scold.
Virgin white, sienna, tarnished brass,
campaign for the analytic resurrection
            of Mademoiselle Malo, a young lady of parts.

Midtown Home

Snow falls so rarely nowadays, and in the city
you miss that sudden whiteness of things.
So when it started in the afternoon I was on the phone
every half hour, arguing with the weather girl
and by dusk there was a good white layer on the streets
and rooftops so that in the blue twilight
the city didn't look so much like the city.

And you need it that way sometimes, especially
in January. I went out into it
and down the corridor of alleys to the park
to watch the conservatory students
slide down the walks and into the dry fountain.
The green bronze nymph was doing that backbend contortion
in a coat of snow, the same way she does it

stark naked in springtime, and with leaves
on her breasts and forehead in autumn. The bronze
war heroes were reserved. But I'm sure
they must love the weather as much as I do,
and wonder why it snows so rarely these days.
I wasn't in such a hurry to get home, with night ahead,
blue light turning to red and then yellow

city light made brighter by the snow,
and I was looking in one back window and then another
all along the brick walls of the alley.
There was this square building with green shades in the windows
making tall white frames of light.
And I saw through a crack the sheets and rails of beds,
but nothing in them, looked like maybe

a hospital supply house? I went closer and there
on the nearest bed just under the window
was half a man's leg and a toothless mouth above it.

And his was only the beginning
        of a row of mouths in shrunken heads,
skins stretched thin and shining over sharp bones,
and limbs and the odds and ends of limbs, like

an ancient tribe disjointed in a higher world
        had spilled into the beds of this crowded home.
I stood trembling in pride and a deeper shame
that with all their futile suffering, borrowed breath,
I held more life in my body than they shared
        in that littered room.
They had no business being alive on a night like that.

Judge Wingate's Lament

Nine killers I sent to the chair, in my youth, nine
          pennies in the fuse box of the law.
One willed me his wooden leg before he sat down
and prayed that I would need it before long.
God save a judge from makeshift religions of the damned.
I am weary of curses and executions.

Jockey

after the fourth race at Laurel

Money talks, but Jack your twenty bucks
        won't make my horses talk.
You take me for another two-bit tout
who haunts the stables shifty-eyed
looking for high-priced nags that run outclassed?
I'll drink with you, but keep that roll in your pants.
Read the scratch sheets
and play some handicapper's tip.
                                        Or if you've got the heart
blow the whole wad on a long shot and be done.

Straight Bourbon. You are a gentleman.
You look me in the eye. And yet you see this
hump that bends my body like an overloaded branch:
it didn't come from pitching hay
or shoveling shit from the paddock to the barn.
This backpack started as a jockey's crouch
        to hide from the wind that fights your stride.
I was light but held my horse's sides
                                        between my legs like a vise,
broke fast and rode hard for the rails,
had my share of the winners but loved them all.
I was the horse's mind, he was my heart.

Then I rode a doctored bay at Pimlico
                        some millionaire had high-nerved for a race,
deadened her leg so she'd run free of the pain.
Well, she ran like a champ until the foreleg snapped
in the backstretch with the grandstand thundering, I went down
under the hooves of those nags she'd left behind.
One beat my shoulder like a gob of dough
                                                and it began to rise.

So the stable was through with me,
the horse-faced women who take the jockey to bed
for a tip and a hard ride,
and tall jades who long to mother a boy-sized man.
Yet I rode for love of the horses, maybe
I'm worth more to them from the ground
than I ever was from their backs.

You know you're betting on a field of cripples
that should be scratched and set to graze?
Look how that roan bolts and halts when he's walked:
he's run his race in the paddock.

That grey has grown boxing-glove ankles.
I've had him stand
all afternoon in a tub of ice to shrink them down.
Another horse runs so doped with azium
he'll run in a dream
and win or lose in a dream.

So you take me for a hunchback fool
because I still won't take you for your money.
Well then lay it on the line.
The measure of a man is the speed
his dream races through the world. You bet
dead money because your life isn't gamble enough.

See that chestnut mare in the ring—
no daisy cutter, she has a great heart to ride;
when she gallops it's a song and you feel
steel springs under you, standing at the rail.
I rode her mother fifteen years ago,
a bright bay dream of sixteen hands,
Cloudland by Wrack out of Fairy Ray by Radium.

Nocturne

1

Moonlight, sly weaver and loom of my sunflower,
            darkness has found you out,
midnight and the night-vision of lovers.
I am on the street in the greater darkness of man-made light,
            a watchman working the graveyard shift.
I'm a safe-cracker tunneling underground dreams,
a second-story man
        flying owl-wise on a draft of nightmares.
You were burning the midnight oil, my pale conspirator,
            and got caught in the act.

By night and the powers of darkness
                I am making a day to live in.
I will gather a dawn from this running starlight.
From glittering eyes of street women, gambler's sweat,
and the final tears of a kidnapped boy in an alley
        I will stitch a fine dew for my lawn.
Sunflowers shall be the light of my garden,
                woven in secrecy, the moon's genius.

2

Grand and eternal creator! Hand
    that spun out the fine rage of the hummingbird,
eye that winked the ox-eye daisy into bloom, you
who pitch the sky tent and drive golden pegs at the horizon—
if I haven't time enough for you in this world
    it's not that I don't care.
My beloved creator, you have not lived in my house.
The one I'm building isn't finished yet.
There are few enough signs of you in the room that I rent.
So, with humility, I am taking
            certain matters of creation into my feeble hands.

How shall I make my city?
I shall build with granite stones and blocks of mud,
I shall frame with a plank of oak and a beaverboard,
                    windowless walls and windows without walls.
I shall nail with galvanized steel and rusted iron.
I shall build the square shells for snails
          and monuments to Federalist pride and Victorian fear.
I shall let the strong stand
               and topple weak structure with my wrecking balls.

3

I am building a song to live in
                    and how shall I make my people?
There will be men of iron and men of tin,
               women of brick and women of blue slate,
people of clay and people of straw,
                         wooden ornament and gold.
I shall make my people the same substance as their dwellings
                    and the spirit of their songs.

No man or woman shall hold public office
                 who is not in the grace of God and the nine muses,
who cannot sing and pray.
No man shall sweep the streets with the great-wheeled carts
who does not love a clean street and the song of the great wheel.
No woman shall bring a child into the world
                         who does not know the song of creation.

What am I bid for my handiwork, my white elephant?

Who am I kidding?
                         I'm the luckiest man in the world
if I can give it away.
                         I see one taker:

Lady, you promised me more than a mortal can pay.
You, woman, you know who I'm talking to.

I have given you jade trinkets and opal rings,
                    the second for bad luck, the first for good.
If I am the source of all riches, don't take advantage.
If I am the final source of evil,
                    take back this talisman you gave me
in a time of true sympathy for my innocent fear.

4

Moonlight, sly weaver and loom of my sunflower,
                    all that is good in me loves darkness,
all that is evil loves the light.
If I have not given the truth then tell me
what is the truth, and if I have not made good
my promises, then what have I done?

                I have driven a thousand miles after her
                        and I have left her alone.

I have loved three women well and some dozen
        better than we deserved.
Now I'd give the whole storm of them and their long memories
      for one who would hold me
through this single night.

From *No Vacancies in Hell* (1973)

for Carolyn Monka

Al Que Quiere

Honor I have none but love plenty.

Sometimes like a monk shot out of his cave,
inner eye dead set on a starred chalice,
silver thistle points,
bright streaks pulse in the distance
above all distance. Or more like

some grizzled trapper come
down out of the barren crags for supplies,
wrapped in fox-skin, bobcat, and ermine,
shocked by the cold and the hard lights of town.
Beating at the doors of old friends

that open a crack and slam. Each year
I have less to give them.
I stop young women in the streets
and ask my most precious questions.
And they ask in return, nothing,
and even this is too much.

Scorpio

I loved a girl who was in love with death
and made him a song she would not sing to me.
My child lay wound in a golden maze of bunting
in her arms, my gift to her, and a still unopened rose.
These could not match death's promises.

"This year is as hard as life by our calendar,
with a black winter at either end of it.
Oh you that so flatter the mystery
but love your answers more,
if the earth should spin at random in the night
and this high room we lie in turn on its stem,
will you know dawn from evening when we rise?"

"It must be the strength of his arms,"
I said, "and eyes that never turn aside."

"No. It is his silent listening," she replied.

I loved a girl who was in love with death
and made him a song she would not sing to me
or speak, or hum, despite
the knot of promise in the boy child's limbs,
the spiral introversion of the rose.

The Secret

She would not pick up stones
even the most beautiful ones
or keep them, let alone
keep them, they never look
the same on the windowsill, or in
a bowl as in the brook,
she would not
pick flowers either
and they grow
so much faster than stones.

Corona

Telling you my love is like trying
to describe the sun in detail,
and it blots hell out of the picture.
Threshed gold. Threshold of your hair,
sun-bedazzled, be-damned, like trying

like a child Sherlock holding the lens above a leaf
at noon, diamond-like convergence on this dot
that saffrons a halo at the edges, then
browns, and a splash of ink-blot shaped space
where the shot blade frazzles and turns back.

Yet if the sun goes out of its way, braiding the best
rays into my lady's hair and makes her shine, who
am I to deny or make light of this, old lover
or new? Clouds hang rain-prone and the sun
opens itself to us only a handful of times:

hold them hard love, and you might not hear
behind you, the nimbus detonating rapid-fire.

Celeste

No fair end to the madder blue of your eyes,
blue currents of your veins race through my sheets
and these wholly unaccountable passions:
a brace of tigers pawing at the stars.

Though we may find no moment right
for death where we go walking,
murder, Celeste, is on my mind,
your life not worth its image on my blade.

The Last Look

When you left in October, I slept
three nights in my clothes to keep the chill away.
Then so many lives passed I can't count them,
ambiguous dawns and sunsets,
the figure's outline on the moonlit beach
in shadowy motion looked the same
wading in, or out of the sea. And you lived
lives apart from me, I remembered all but that
you are a woman. In August you returned, unfaithful,
my dream of you, a blue-white star
frozen in a ripple of ice, shattered.
A fist rammed through the window pane,
blood stained the silver spiderweb of cracks,
slivers, as in the old wives' tale
rushed upstream to the heart. Forgive me,
I was a child again, left a dead man's problem,
tears the only sign of life on a barren face.
When all I could feel for you was a cool rain
lightening the ponderous thunder in my heart.

The Search

In my new house, windows at eyelevel
with the sun at dusk stare hard at me,
lone gull in a glass maze
beating limp wings against the solid glare.
Landlocked. I haven't been able to feel at home
and your letter ripped open on my desk
asking me to look for you, set me crazy.

For a day you were here five days ago,
the spray of purple ironweed
browns in an earthen jug with two other wildflowers
you picked, whose names I have forgotten.
I have forgotten your names, those
given you by love, and I'm lost,
lone fool in a glass cage,
disjointed puppet hanging in a jar deadpan,
our loves of the past fall so far behind me
that the brightest leaf now descending
will not touch warm ground.

A night of sitting alone, falling
asleep, falling into tears
until the moon through the broken window grew
transparent, lost its edge
and the craters flooded with skylight.
You were the only shadow thrown on my body
at daybreak, when the mist uncovered
fields splashed red with poppies, flying. Catch
hold!
            I cannot speak in miracles, Pamela,
pin-point, counterpoint
the shifting center of flawless crystal
where we stood. You must look for yourself.

Lady in Her Bath

All day has been morning. Birds rattle,
the trees stock still beneath them,
leaves blue in the white air. The girl bathes
gracefully, her own epiphany,
all of cool circles in water.
Does a god move in her limbs or is there
a god in the air around her guiding them? Or
is all light self-radiant?

She draws her body slowly through the pool
bathing him from her, his flesh
and vision. It is this freedom
that is divine in her momentarily,
flash of her smooth limbs, white, whole.

The eyes are violet. Her eyes are blue,
yet bathing, the bright sun
deepens them. The eyes are her own,
not violet for nothing. I will leave out
the lips, for these the light has forgotten.

Requiem for Christine Latrobe

> And we will all be together in torment and so we will not need to remember love and fornication, and maybe in torment you cannot remember why you are there. And if we cannot remember all this, it can't be much torment.
>
> —FAULKNER

Tragic wisteria nodding compassionate
lighter-than-lilac heads, bindweed, convolvulus,
you too to be reckoned with. Perverse,
flourishing at dockside to beat Hell. I am unsure
you are not spirits transplanted from some
careless purgatory short on space. I suspect
your flowers whirled first out of the sea mist
then the umbilical vine
last shooting its hairy tendrils into the loam.

She loved you like sisters. You would make secrets
of each individual sorrow and hide them all
so, in that camouflage of constant mourning,
as darkly for a thousand colorless corpses as for none
run aground on the Patapsco banks.
Coast guardsmen root them up out of the sand,
jerk back the drenched heads by the hair and leave them
unidentified, faces worn smooth
as quartz rubbed pearly at a creek's bottom.

One of those wrecks I hereby claim
while scavengers claw the sandbars for a shell.
Our single spirit is fit to be tied
with my shiftless half of its body still at large.

In that house skirted with green awnings, in the room
with awnings that looms above the harbor, shady-eyed
like a visored money-changer in a penny arcade,
they have gathered to find you dead there,

the prolix and fugitive tenses of your soul
finally calm and collected. Puffed eyes
of the matrons run, the lids rubbed raw
with mascara grit, men's cambric
handkerchiefs soggy with sweat. Over the door
a stone cross-eyed screech owl winks from the spandrel.

There will be words. And none of them
will dare the truth, that they were not robbed
merely of the corpse, but that for sure
no respectable death would visit there
to flatter that coffin of flame-grained mahogany
prone on the pallet, vacant and gutless, or add
a faint bloom to the steaming rose's cheek.
They would have doctored the honest death out of her,
injected a bloodless smile into the lips
and stretched her out in effigy. Better lost,
seaweed winding the swollen veins,
eye sockets granulated with sand-pulver, the clabber flesh
pickled in natural solutions.
They don't care what death is or what it means.

There is so much I fear
you would not dare. I fear your soul
evaporated from the earth half-heartedly
leaving a sea-nettle grey residue
adrift in this heaving backwash still sensate.
And I keep fumbling after your last wishes.
Did they drive at death head-on
or finally turn, tug shyly at his sleeve,
the pain of fear outscreaming all the pain
that sent you there? But death holds out
its crash course, for authentic inductees,
in the language of unearthly things. Tottering
with you on the wire I may share

the nightmare of your fall, as unsure
of my next breath. Yet I'm denied the last
flash that burns all shadows from the truth before
you land wide of the last-minute net.

Rust-bound dredges in the harbor-mouth,
barges girded with black links of tire bumpers,
slanted derricks tilting at the sun.
Watching along the pine-cord wharves
for that sign you promised you would send
when the good times had all gone out of us.
But there are so many yours might be
lost in the rush or is it that
the time still hasn't come? We have promised
and been sworn so many things.
I may not have believed you when it came.

I have gone out in the streets looking for it,
peeping through newssheets riddled at the seams,
an apprentice hawkshaw periscoping street corners
with half an eye. The shrill vendor parading
his mare-drawn cart stacked with yam-crates, strawberries,
bumped on his good leg swinging a cloth-yard of space
from the street to a nervous thigh stump;
a blind drunk murmured into an ash-can
trying to wake an echo up
from the pit of dead metal—any ghost of a voice
not his own—that might
make loneliness something other than just
talking to himself. I heard this dream
turned on with a mystical hymn-like resonance
and lost bitching in the cavernous drum.
And turned back to the waterfront with no more sense
than those professional mourners of what was lost

and a damned sight less
idea what deserves the curse of being forgotten.

When time dies I know every second of it
must rattle off into Hell
for reminding men what is never too soon
wrecked and done with. I take it all back,
all my lies against your will,
though there were times when the gods I swear
seemed to whisper through my fingertips, touching you.

The Falls let down its black alluvion
from Harford Run to South Street long ago
hardened the river's arteries, gathering reefs
like broad-cloth ripples when drawn, or each thought
wrinkles its author's forehead, isolate and frail.
High tide swamped these until the shoals
bedded down and fly-by-night islands became fast land.
The brackish stream ran sapphire clear among them
and shark teeth of the schooners' topsails
of Guttro and Blanc, ran, that cut best behind the wind.
Those French merchants your ancestors kept their faith,
driven to each makeshift tabernacle
from the last, by pioneers in God's new holy land.

If your remains demand a charnel house I'll rent
the memory of St. Peter's chapel, snatch it
floating transparent up Charles Street, naked
tracing arrowtip steeples in the air,
and with no walls that stand to contain you.
I would prefer to have us both, who split
the live and dead worlds between us,
knee the rotted altar of some haunted church
in mind, that cannot scare the gods away.

My thought sends word it is hidden in my heart
but does the heart sound empty? What is that light
that shines on / off in the distance so persistently
flickering? Where is the pure mothering black-light of
        grief
that lights bones up from the inside, ultra-violet,
and rots the heart's teeth?

From the spare room of this world
I kept my vigil armed with one frail thought.
Where there is real tragedy is no terror
and no pity. The wild prayers
I have withheld for you
whose longing silence must outdistance death.

Madonna (with Child Missing)

Shouts from the street, spotlights crossfire
at a third story window. The woman
stares through smoked glass at a crowd
and firemen in glazed slickers—
flames climbing the stairs behind her two at a time.
She lifts up the window sash with one hand,
kisses the infant and rolls it out trusting the air,
the soft knock of skull on stone in her heart.

The Jewelsmith's Last Apprentice

No seed of scrap platinum left to spring
light from the crucible's matrix;
I've scraped the chalk-flat porcelain clean,
laid his tools out: copper pickle tongs,
clock tweezers, pitch tongs and the dapping die
nearly leap from the selvedge cloth and shine.
One hour since dawn and the bench is set,
ready for the master when he comes.

Though there's no depending on a man that old
and I might well be sleeping.
Not so much his memory as his life I doubt
today, with this maddening necklace to cast
for the councilman's new lady, whose white throat
blinded the brightest pearls I tested there.
The blue tear of flame that tips the gas torch
goes glassy in the stronger light:

he's late. All I can do is save his steps,
leave no quarrel for his hands
that mine might settle, set out the vials
of ground cobb, that bleeds the sweat out of the gold,
steel shot for roughing the stones slick, enamels
that whirl a pinwheel palette in the brain,
sheepskin and canton flannel buffs
that tickle the delicate rubies into flame.

What time's lost makes work the longer, I must
set all the matter closer to his mind,
let the stones loose, save him the detail
of folding and unfolding diamond paper, fiddling
locks, the numbers click off in my head,
there—four turns and tumblers trip, the crossbar falls!
Two black boxes slide from a deeper vault,
jewels wrapped square in glazed tissues crackling

in my fingers under the arclight, sapphires
from Kashmir, chipped off a brick of fallen heaven
in late evening when planets glow dim,
amethysts strained from violet-stained sand
in Rio Grande do Sul, pigeon-blood rubies.
And like stars sprung from glass uncracked by hail,
the shivering wreckage of some mad god's ideal,
diamonds whose cold sparkling stings your eye.

What will suit this lady? I heard
her ask for a corsage of violets and musk rose
in cold stones; if she knew
how tortuously the bush these grow from breeds!
They ask for the sudden flush of the true rose
without penalty of death wish or thorn.
Let's have an emerald for each mistress that she rivals,
a string of duck bone jade and blister pearls.

There will be little left for him to do
if my piece displeases him. He shouldn't be
so old as to forget that he is old and leave
a young man waiting hot to take his place.
So I am master of this work, unchallenged,
but where is my apprentice? Off
to steal the lady that it's fashioned for?
There's no relying on tomorrow's youth.

If she could know who had transformed
in one lightning collision all this gold and silver
to a battle of the sun and moon,
and the sky blown wide with stars!
The necklace must burn low on her breasts,
with such sweat my hands have bent the yielding gold,
how could she not love me feeling
the press of my passion and genius in its shape?

Miss Ellie's 78th Spring Party

Miss Ellie rattles the champagne glasses
like crystal ghosts that tinkle when they touch,
to hail the Main Line in for Spring
at the last minute. There isn't much
time to call the company to come;
this year she has forgotten everything.

Picasso's dancers shiver in a frame
next to the window. Spring as well
seems to have forgotten itself.
Several curios upon the shelf,
a lion and a girl in porcelain,
tumbled when an icy draft rained in.

She wondered for a moment who would come
this year; though she'd forgotten, who'd recalled?
She forgot again what day it had become.
All the tenses moved two ways at once,
past and present standing back to back
moved through each other with no deference
to Spring or Miss Ellie. She is young and old
alike and won't remember which is when.
The company will be arriving soon
                                                            and then
everyone has gone off in the cold.

Fire froze in the chimney. The first cork
exploded from the bottles, aimed to blast
a marble frieze of Pan upon the stair
and everyone who ever was was there
to breathe the spirits moving from the glass.

First Precinct Fourth Ward

Every bar on The Block shut down.
Villa Nova, the Crystal, the Ritz, and Midway,
dead neon, night flowers gone day blind,
eyes like a gutted steeple,
streetwalker with her make-up peeled clean.

The paradise is no more artificial
than the money paid out for it.

Get your morning hotdog at Pollock Johnnie's
but don't ask for a drink.
This is the blade of justice untempered.
No truth in wine?
No more truth anywhere in town:
when a man can't get booze on The Block
at a reasonable hour, or an unreasonable hour,
when a sailor can't go for broke on East Baltimore Street
after a dry month at sea,
when a man can't get shot on East Baltimore Street
for minding someone else's business,
a sailor can't get stoned, layed, and rolled
for his pay
then we must look elsewhere for The Republic.

Blaze Star, where has she gone,
and Lola, that up-side-down girl
and a hundred others that dance the drinks off the bar-tops,
and the topless shoe-shine girls,
and the shades of countless women trapped in the photo
peep shows?
They have all gone to the polls.
Jimmie the Greek is laying one hundred to one
the President can't lose,
and the action is slower than a drugged clock,
and may be slower.
But some people will bet on anything.

Letter Concerning the Yellow Fever

> *The disease called the bilious remittent or Yellow Fever is a disease of climate, unconnected with a foreign origin. This may appear to you as a novel opinion, but my reasons for it are strong and shall be furnished for your consideration if it should please God to spare my life until I have more leisure . . .*

To Edward Johnson, Esquire,
Mayor of the City of Baltimore

September 20th, 1818

Good health to you today sir and excuse
my want of promptness in this hectic time.
Your letter has overtaken me just now, the servant
eased it swift into my pocket
on the stairs to my first sleep these last two nights.
I am just come from the bedside of a girl
late visited with distemper, and have yet
to put her from my thoughts. The eyes bloodshot glared
at me, as though I were to blame
for the barb in her liver and gum swelled in her jaw.
And when I thumbed her eyelid back upon the ball,
the tongue lay so foul in the gutter of her mouth
I bid her clamp the lips over her teeth
to spare us the dread vapour.
She threw herself from side to side in bed,
her head like a coin just knocked and slowed
from its upright spin. I swear sir
I could hear her heart beat cross the room,
yet had to pinch her wrist for the softest pulse.
I drew thirty ounces of blood at a bleeding
to unfold the circulation and as mean
to the operation of her medicine:
six grains of tartar steeped in bone set tea,

spiritus mindereri cut with sweet spirit of nitre
and black snake root tea to open wide her pores.
I must return there in four hours time
between moon-set and day-break to see
what miracle I've worked.
Twixt now and then I'll set down all I can.

You know the great body of this city stands
on high and commanding ground, rolling
south where the land's peak stabs into Morgan's Cove,
the jagged outline of the wharves
like the apothecary's drachm mark *in extenso.*
So you see we are almost completely surrounded by water.
In summer such rank miasma clouds the point
that all but true natives of the Block are forewarned
to pinch ground garlic and shag tobacco up the nose
to choke back poison that would enter there.
Each June they scare some novel scapegoat:
ten years ago the pumping of bilge water and discharge
of ballast from the ship United States
that festered bare in the sun's eye near Pitt Street.
Now they accuse a parcel of putrid wheat
passed by when a ship's cargo was hauled ashore,
and left to soak in brine flooding the hold.
These are the same philosophers who chew
peach sprouts for ague, and probe their carious teeth
with splinters of sycamores struck low by lightning,
certain the charred pick must kill the nerve!
Next they'll blame the rotting carcass
of some dog rolled by schoolboys in the mud
or a poor hump-backed hag
who's let her wash hang out too long.
Yet give ear to these, sir,
for they are not so wide of the mark
as certain of your august professionals.

I beseech your patience for what gall
may color a weary man's pen scrawl at midnight.
We would gladly set all blame for this horror
on our remotest enemy. Yet those
who have scouted its trail through the body
and plotted its terrible course on the map of land
know that the plague thrives in isolation,
is seasonal, and brewed at home.
Now certain high medical authorities
who sit down in their closets
and wrap up nonsense into an imposing shape,
will declare the wharves merely the lobby of contagion,
an innocent port where the alien disease puts in
to be distributed like so much freight.
These are sly tricksters wooing
our dull eyes to the shining goose in one hand
that will become a buzzard in the other,
whisking us past that black veil of exchange.

Two hundred tallied dead there in a week.
Those of us who schemed
to cheat the fever of its crop took note
of an uncommon green cast
to the dock waters in the plague's rage.
And an odor of cold damp cellars, putrid fish
or fowl's entrails rose from the water
like steam from a bubbling cistern.
We judged this a species of vile vegetable ferment
(you've seen how short a time it takes
wood to spice fresh water in a clean bucket?)
and ordered the harbour's derelicts towed and burned,
decaying arcs, hulks, masts, and spars.
Yet this failed to slow the fever's pace
and all our wreckers caught the plague and died.

We did not know as yet the very earth
we walked upon was poisoned. The streets
of Fell's Point, the wharves and dock abutments all ride
on low new-made ground, on loan
from marsh-water and drowned wood at a high rate.
Sir, to make ground the way they do
is more perilous than to raise battlements
on layers of dry dirt and gunpowder!
Way out in the harbour they drive a circle of piles,
then choke the pit with green saplings and pine cord wood,
pine tops, old barrels, chips and sawdust, shavings,
veneered with a thin green sodded stratum of earth.
The redskins might have made a better job of it
who would have left it to God,
who would have put it off indefinitely.
God knows we have less use for man-made land
than any tribe of men who ever lived.

As for the doctrine of contagion!
Those idle speculators who deal in it
for their share of the merchant's profit
will have a dead cart creaking under the weight
of this strange species of harvesting
to carry with them to the courts above. Although
perhaps they can gain no case so priceless
as that when the Yellow Fever was blown
from the docks to the senate chamber in Charlestown,
striking the winded delegates down in midspeech
until they lacked quorum. The survivors then
entertained the motion of abandoning
a country on which the judgements of heaven
must fall with so heavy a hand.

Yet such faith the people have in your provision,
they would have a man whipped through the streets

who would charge you with starting at a phantom
while a flesh and blood demon lodges in your house.
Why do they expect you to be versed
in those coy arcana of nature, heavenly laws
that strongarm matter, constant in causes
both friendly in man, and fatal?
You know no more of sickness than the wheelwright
who knows only when he is well,
no more than a carpenter knows of law
and the benign herding of men, who feels it
only when his next peg-nail is taxed out of reach.
But will men have you to hang the effluvia
between heaven and earth for a season
and give it no true origin—no progenitor—no abode
thereafter—neither author nor finisher?
Will you sit back and fold your arms, resigned
that he is a "demon that moves in darkness,"
contenting yourself to do nothing
because he is sometimes merciful?

I fear you haven't drawn
the circle of your advisors wide enough, or that
you have let treacherous quacks hang on your ear:
perhaps the leeches of a group of merchants
who have something more at stake
in this matter than their lives, or the lives
of anyone, and who beside
maintain estates for refuge in the county?
Well let them mark they look not far enough
in their own interests! Would they choose
to pick the pockets of rank corpses
and worry with dusting the wallets with gunpowder
to singe clean the money they infected first?

Lately a milliner sent
his apprentice to call on a shopkeeper in arrears.
Three times the boy knocked hard at the oak door,
that opened at length on a man with death in his face.
And when the child recited the sum of money owed,
this living ghost replied:
"call as you go by at Cripplegate Church
and bid them ring the bell," and with this said,
he shut the door, stomped up the stairs and died.

Sir I would train the coldest eye on all of this
as befits the case at large,
but for those cases we cannot serve without
recall to the roots of passion. These sprout alike
into the quick of each of us, in a few certain ways,
though our faces reveal only the flower and leaf.
A happy loophole in the contract
designed to make each man his best friend's mystery,
most fortunate for our craft!
For we are men first that we might become physicians,
and never turn the balance of this debt.

It is late at night or I would blot much out
and pen this whole epistle over again.
No shriveled crone schooled in backwoods witchery
or drunken sexton who's a friend to death
eyes my skill with such high contempt as life itself.
My hand always trembles when I attend her alone,
as now, with no struggling flesh there to distract me.
She smiles when I instruct her how to live.
Do not smile. There's not one man sick
but an entire city, and the plague threatens to leave
us without lives enough to bear the dead away.

I urge in short
you bid the merchants wall their docks in granite,
and burn some three dozen ships—
the poison greases their hulls like green sea-slime.
Let the pigs and cattle loose to root in the streets,
and discharge cannon at the break of day
where miasma is thickest, to shake it from the air.
Then there is that passage of Leviticus. Good health
to you again sir! I must return
before there is light to see my next patient dead.

William Martin
Fell's Point, Baltimore

The Assassins

(Easter Monday 1865)

Thomas! I warn you
whistle twice from the high road—
I sleep with this pistol in my grip,
sleep less and less, dream none and wake up hard.
And the pain in my leg has run from a slow throb
to fits of shuddering in the damp.
A fine job he did, the good doctor,
the son of a bitch, if he didn't
set the bone to knit askew,
then turns me out to pitch in this gangrened sluice
and rest my head on a cold stone.

Pour me a half cup of brandy there
and take a short one to the boy.
        You see him through the laurel on his knees?
He hasn't moved for hours, and when I call
he starts and gapes as if I were a ghoul
or harpy riding the late-night post from Hell.
        He will not drink? Well let him freeze.
His bent limbs will make fine woodland statuary
and put to shame
any limp-necked puppet dangling from a noose.
He served me well, Thomas, served me well.
Unroll the newsheets from your saddlebag
and hook the lantern on that hanging cedar branch.

Look here—they've sighted, handcuffed, or shot down
a dozen counterfeits of me today,
the leg fractured in as many different places,
mustache peeled from the lip.
        What man is man enough to grant my courage
is welcome to the fame. They wrong me.
The Yankees nod and dip their pens, headline

the wild cortege of my ancestry
(they're satisfied I'm lunatic by blood),
and cry "coward," black-tongued in the iron presses.
        No courage crusades outside of their law.
I wonder what the Richmond paper says.
They never praised my acting in the North.

They are an audience of basilisks
that drags to the theatre as some grave black mass
and won't sit still for any scene that lives.
No romance or heart-sound tragedy;
give them a dance of death or miracle play,
some tableau to stretch the conscience on the rack.
I played the scene they craved, to a broken tune,
dry organ snatches of the Miserere
that wailed from a hundred church doors at His death:
raw meat for the kites of guilt-scarred memory.
And still they carp and hiss. We cannot please.

And what man was this to name their God on earth,
who wears black gloves to the opera in New York
and has black guests to dine at the White House?
They would have made that bearded spider their next God
who dresses always in mourning.
I fear I might have played into their hands
by martyring him. Yet better
a martyr dead in heaven before his time
than a saint strutting the earth above the law.

That boy will deafen the delicate ear of heaven,
he prays with such a vengeance. And you know
he begs for nothing of good use.
For how could a merciful God deny
such devotion, and for what other kind
would Harold cramp his arms and legs that long?
Yet there he kneels, as if his only wish

were that he might continue praying there.
    What do you pray for Harold?
For your saviour to return to earth,
or for a place in some less clamorous Hell
where the katydids and birds are bound and gagged?

Oh Katy shall be free tonight and sing in the sycamores!
How you can banish sleep, quiet, and good temper,
oh Katy how many nights have you kept me awake
cursing your strange monotonous shrill song!
    Now what do you pray for Harold,
do you want a place in history or in heaven,
a world of stress and battle and rare glory
or that tedious paradise for saints
turned out to pasture, the white celestial jail
of pitiless harmony?
Look how his hands tremble
welded at his palms, useless,
useless. No prayer will make them one.

Jimsonweed and belladonna grow at my side.
And I have watched the red-tailed hawk at dusk
wheeling his watch above the black-slash pines,
and yellow flickers in the buckthorn.
And I half expect some marvelous thought to pass
where never a thought has been before,
to shiver my soul like a wine glass, flawed and frail
screamed at by a high-strung violin.
    Oh Thomas you have lived
and taken life where it was not freely given:
what worth is the judgement of God or men,
what plush heaven or hell's broil, bribe or threat,
once a man has bought and paid for his own soul?

We dare not stir until the search moves north.
You must inquire where a man might send

word of an assassin's whereabouts
after the troops decamp from Nanjemoy.
If you should corner the major where he drinks
or meet him through the local whores,
don't look eager or you will be known outright.
He'll have learned of your former rebel sympathies
and distrust a sudden change of heart.
Act more as if you couldn't give a damn
to cling to some bygone dream
when there's a solid profit to be made.
No man will guess you would do otherwise.

They say who breaks the silence feels
the brush of an angel's wing.
I know there are no angels in this grove.
Your paper says the mark of Cain is on my brow
though not one of us has an eye for it.
And I'm damned for the deed that honored Brutus.
They've put a handsome price on my head, more money
than three virtuous men make in a lifetime.
I swear I would rather see an honest cutthroat
grow fat on my useless flesh
than a trigger-happy deacon drunk on the voice of God.
How can you afford not to betray me?

The Exile's Letter

I first left the cities behind, then
the crowded wheat-fields, and last the women
because I couldn't bear their loneliness.
Far away they spin, behind me,
and the stuttering bells and hysterical sirens
speed out of earshot
wailing like deserted children.

Heaven still lies far beyond my means,
there are no vacancies in hell—
no goddamned place to go now,
not one blessed thing left to do.

And at this distance I'm no better
than a punch-drunk photographer, scrambling
in widening circles at a family reunion,
up and down on one knee,
telescoping the clustered generations
and defying their forced gravity.

Bodies crammed near static in the streets
await the plague winds of late spring:
cool air of death to stave off famine,

while I'm land-wrecked a few miles from water
feeling more happiness than they can know,
hoping that one straw of sunlight piercing a cloud
can prop the sky up for a few more hours.

Song of the Beekeeper

My bees gather the last winter store
from smart-weed. Spanish needles goldenrod.
        I will have my cup right side up
            when the hives rain honey,
and men in town will pay for it.
        They are afraid of the sting.
When I'm wiring the brood comb frames
        and folks ask my business, tell them
I'm stringing the harp for my bees.

Song of the Sap Miller

Give us a southwest wind after the frost
            to set my trees all tingling in the grain.
Sun draw the sap up
                        frost keep it down:
    no sap before light hits the frost,
    no sap when the cold is gone.
Kettles hang in the granite arch,
            a blue stream of smoke twisting skyward.
Smooth-skinned young maples start with high spirit,
fair on a run and flooding the keelers,
but they won't hold out.
    Now my thick-barked scarlet ladies
            do not shy at my auger.
I'll sink the elder spiles no deeper
    than your sweet white wood
and tickle the juice from your limbs.

Song of the Young Woman Gathering Ginseng*

I've been hunting ginseng since dawn
        from Sang Run to Backbone Mountain
untangling brush under red oak trees.
This virgin bed blooms with the five-fingered leaves,
and the berries! A berry for every flower.
My skirt is full of the spiral trunks, some
heart-shaped roots for the heart, spindles
that grind well for herb tea. But you
        little man, with your broad shoulders
and long taproot legs, you will bring
a pretty penny in the Chinese market.
Some lord will bid high to feel you under his belt.

* An herb found in the Allegheny Mountains, long prized by the Chinese for its curative and aphrodisiac properties.

Night Song from Backbone Mountain

Because you threw rocks at me on Backbone Mountain,
called me skinhead and my dog a bowlegged weasel,
don't come looking for me here to make up.
Go dig your own groundnuts if you can find them
    and onion weeds, and I hope
you choke on the buckbeans.

I'm nobody's fool, Jim Lewis.
I saw you lay her on the ground,
    your hands tangled up in her hair.
I saw you and I tried to run away
        up to Devil's Rock, up there
I watched her lead you back to town.

That is her way. I'm nobody's fool.
I know every bird here every leaf by names
    I gave them out of love, not
some name I stole from a book.
Every night I see the sun down
(you told me not to stare into the sun

    but still I go right on),
and I know my way by the stars.
No deer runs from me or wild turkey.
I live, I have been happy.
I'm nobody's fool but suppose I was
    and you were dead right all along?

A slant-toothed fool has his glory
    when banjos pick up in the bar,
and he dances for what dimes men toss on the floor.
They're his when he's done and gone home.
    So long Jim Lewis.
I have been happy, so long.

Patty Cannon

Moon spun full in cold April,
frost on the blue-black skins
shivering chains in a thicket
of blackjack oak and white pine.

Cyrus Bell sailed up from Norfolk,
his satchel bulging with gold
to buy Patty Cannon's bootleg slaves
and smuggle them south in the hold.

Cyrus Bell rapped at Patty's door,
she led him down the hall.
"Could you trouble to put me up?" he winked.
"No trouble for me at all."

She set him a place at the window
to look on the dark broad yard;
she drew him an amber dram of rye
and set it down hard on the board.

"Those are stars that dance in the treetops,
it's too early for fireflies;
and those lights that glint in the underbrush
are whites of the black men's eyes."

Cyrus Bell peered into the darkness
while Patty went for bread
she went for a matchlock pistol too
and buried a ball in his head.

She sacked his pockets and satchel
and carved him limb from limb;
she took him apart like a puppet
to fold in a chest of pine.

The chest was carved and painted
blue and glittering gold;
she dug him a grave in the April ground
and lowered him down in the cold.

She lowered him down in the April ground
and kept her slaves and the gold,
she dropped the chest and stamped the earth
but the grave didn't hold.

A ploughman was tearing the damp sweet ground,
cutting a trench for his seed
when the spring-toothed harrow kicked and snagged
on Cyrus Bell's death bed.

Patty is gone to the Georgetown jail
and a crowd trails howling behind.
She lies chained in the cold cell, curses
drift through the bars on the wind.

A good horse will see death in the distance,
a crow talks if you split his tongue,
streaks of light the clouds let through are pipes
drawing water to the sun.

Patty Cannon kept locked in an amulet,
a vial of black widow tea;
"If God hasn't struck me dead," she swore,
"no man will ever hang me."

Wild geese fled screaming the fallen sun
afire behind the mist.
The sun was done for, the western sky
held a glowing coal in its fist.

Song of the Hermit

Traveler beware, your cool grottos
hollowed in the world's side are my anterooms.

Sing clear of my range
or hear your song die fast on the air
like breath that clouds in the cold and vanishes.

There is no walking shadow in these hills
but mine; my dreams are singular.

ACKNOWLEDGMENTS

Grateful acknowledgment is made to the editors of the following magazines, in which these poems first appeared: *Agenda* (England), *Almanaco* (Italy), *America, American Scholar, Atlanta Review, Atlantic Monthly, Chelsea, Dalhousie Review* (Canada), *Georgia Review, Hudson Review, Kenyon Review, Little Review, Michigan Quarterly, Narrative, Nation, National Review, New Criterion, New Republic, New York Sun, New Yorker, North American Review, OnEarth, Open City, Paris Review, Per Contra, Poetry Magazine, Prairie Schooner, Raritan, Sewanee Review, Shenandoah, Southern Review, Southwest Review,* and *Virginia Quarterly.*

The sonnets in *Cruel April: Poems from the Pandemic* are the text of a film directed by Douglas Trapp, in which the actors Tyne Daly, Paul Hecht, Jennifer Van Dyck, and Harris Yulin recite the sonnets over a montage of art and photography from the Tivoli Gallery, New York. The short film is available online.

"Jacob at Peniel" is the text for a ballet that was performed by Momentum Dance Company in 1985.

The Italian translation by Simone Dubrovic of "Water Lilies," from the sequence "Homage to Mallarmé" (from *Dall'alba al Crepuscolo-Poesie 1967–2014,* Raffaelli Editore, Rimini 2020), inspired the harp sonata "Le Ninfee," by Harpist Emanuela Battigelli. It was recorded on Battigelli's CD *Le Ninfee* (Artesuono, 2020). I am grateful to Mr. Dubrovic for his skillful translation of my *Selected Poems,* and to Ms. Battigelli for her beautiful harp piece.

"Autumn Song" was performed on NPR's *The Writer's Almanac.*

"Miss Ellie's 78th Spring Party" and "The Sentry of Portoferraio" first appeared in *New Yorker.* "The Comb-Bearers" first appeared in *Poetry Magazine.* "Climbing," "Cygnus Musicus," "The Follies," "The Inheritance," "Miami," "The Man without Legs," "Mannequins," and "Phidias in Exile" first appeared in *American Scholar.*

NOTES

"The Gulf Stream": The image from Winslow Homer's painting is well-known.

"The Pessimism of Richard Porson": Richard Porson (1759–1808), English classical scholar.

"To Richard Wilbur": Richard Wilbur (1921–2017), an American poet.

"A Dream": Ford Madox Ford (1873–1939), was an English author and editor.

"Journal of the Plague Year" uses phrases from Defoe's book of the same name.

"Paulinus of Nola" (354–431 A.D.): A Roman poet and friend of the poet Ausonius, to whom this Latin poem is addressed.

"Dawn to Twilight": The poem is inspired by Victor Hugo's famous "Demain, dès l'aube." "Autumn Song" and the refrain from "He Wanted to Travel" owe a debt to Jean-Baptiste Chassignet.

"Psalm of Pernette Du Gillet" is a close translation of the untitled "La nuit était pour moi si très-obscure," written by the poet Pernette Du Guillet (c. 1520–1545). She is said to be the real-life inspiration for Maurice Scève's sequence of love poems "Delia: The Paragon of Virtue." She died in her twenties. The "broken gate" is my embellishment.

"Tornado, 1911": A similar incident was reported in the *Yorkshire Observer* on February 25, 1911. The report was subsequently redacted by William Godden in *Symons's Meteorological Magazine* 46:54, 1911.

"On a Theme of Ronsard": This theme appears throughout Pierre de Ronsard's works but is especially focused in his poem "À Philippes des-Portes, Chartrain. Elegie," published in 1587.

"Eurylochus Recalls the Sirens": The speaker, or writer, Eurylochus, was one of the crew on the ship that sailed near the island where the Sirens' songs lured mariners to their deaths. Brave Odysseus was so curious about the singing that he had himself lashed to the mast, his ears unstopped, while the other mariners plugged their ears with wax. Eurylochus tells the story from his point of view; despite the wax, he recalls enough of the singing to describe it.

"The Lightning and the Key": I have often been asked to provide context for the dramatic monologues that have played such a significant role in my books, just as I would do if I were reading them aloud to an audience. This poem is an imagined letter from Ben Franklin's son, the notorious Loyalist William Franklin, in 1802. It is written to his old friend, the English scientist Joseph Priestly. Both men are in exile: Franklin in England, for his loyalty to the Crown during the American revolution; Priestly in America, driven from England because of his sympathies with the French Revolution. The scientist has asked for Franklin's recollection of the famous kite experiment. The request inspires William to tell the tragedy of his life.

"The Ferryman": Lord Dunsany (Edward Plunkett, 1878–1957) was an Irish dramatist and poet.

"Solomon and the Four Winds": A dramatic monologue spoken by Rehoboam, a protégé of his father King Solomon. The speaker, now an old man, is addressing a historian who wishes to record the wisdom of Solomon, and Rehoboam wants to distinguish fact from legend. The tale he chooses to tell, about his own apprenticeship in a court case overseen by his father, is both fantastic and wise. The story is based on a Sephardi Folktale.

"Cygnus Musicus": The swan here is no relation to the real bird, Cygnus Musicus, the Whooper Swan of Europe and Canada. The myth of the Cygnus Musicus was based upon the notion that a creature so beautiful ought to make beautiful music.

"Homage to Mallarmé": These poems were inspired by the prose poems "Plainte d'automne," "Frisson d'hiver," and "Le Nénuphar blanc."

"The Testament of Isaac Lakedion": Lakedion is the legendary Wandering Jew, who witnesses the Crucifixion and upon whom Christ passes the sentence of immortality. He cannot die. As the speaker of this version of the legend, Isaac Lakedion wanders into a ruined synagogue in Baltimore, where he is found by the poet, who takes him home for a night of conversation. The dramatic monologue is addressed by Lakedion to the poet.

"Lafayette Square": The speaker is Clover Adams, the suicidal wife of Henry Adams (1838–1918). She is addressing her husband, the great historian and descendent of two presidents.

"Letter to Thomas Edison from John Burroughs": Burroughs (1837–1921), the distinguished naturalist, is writing to his friend Thomas Edison about their mutual friend, the inventor and capitalist Henry Ford, trying to enlist Edison's aid in saving Ford's soul and his genius from materialism.

"Letter Concerning the Yellow Fever" is a dramatic monologue in the form of a letter from a physician, Dr. William Martin, to the mayor of Baltimore during the Yellow Fever epidemic of 1818, an effort to persuade the city government to clean up the harbor and eliminate the pollution that spawns the disease.

"The Assassins": The speaker is John Wilkes Booth three days after the assassination of Lincoln. His leg is broken. In agony and fury, he is speaking to Thomas Harold, one of his accomplices.

"Patty Cannon" (c. 1760–1829) was an illegal slave trader on the Delmarva peninsula.

INDEX OF TITLES

INDEX OF FIRST LINES